Letters from the Front

Essays for the Unapologetic

©2018 Rachel Summers

Culture and Society

Remembering Your Roots

Red, yellow, orange, and green blur together as I stare into the colorful hills between Brasstown Bald and Blood Mountain, deep in the wilds of North Georgia, the foothills of the Appalachians – and one had better pronounce that with a short *a* around here. I wonder, will these smokey, rolling hills be the last stronghold of Euro-American culture? Ever a retreat for the strong-willed and stubborn, Appalachia is still a hold-out for those who value tradition, heritage, and the tried and true ways of our hardened ancestors. Music, ministry, and moonshine find a place here, unhurried by the rest of the world whose rootless inhabitants see the so-called hillbilly as a backward fool, a caricature of humanity to be mocked and abused without fear of breaking any politically correct taboos.

The hillbilly, the redneck, the backwoods cracker. Who is he? He is a rebel, stubbornly defiant to the tainted gods of progress. He is a man who will fight for freedom, tradition, family. He is a man who remembers. He remembers his ancestors, those rugged frontier farmers who marched westward with their fiddles, forges, and folktales. He remembers their courageous answer to the call for revolution. He remembers their pivotal roll in founding and settling this country. Ask him; the hillbilly remembers.

He remembers his ancestors' reluctance to join in the War between the States; most hill folk were too poor and willfully isolated to care for the politics of the rest of the country and they certainly did not care for the few wealthy planters who might reside nearby. They were drafted just the same, and so they marched out of the mountains and did their duty. How were they rewarded? In the chaotic aftermath of the war we find tales of rebel soldiers just trying to go home and get on with their lives. Sure, the war was over but not for these poor folk; East Tennessee had it the worst.

Governor Brownlow, a Northern interloper, decided to cleanse the mountains because he thought those ungodly rebels, even the women and children, should all be killed and he set about doing just that – and all of this after the war. They were ordered to leave and many did, just loaded their wagons and went west. The ones who stayed and got caught became victims of classic mob mentality, receiving 400 lashes or just plain being shot. If you defended yourself, you were hung. Brownlow even asked citizens and soldiers alike to dispose of rebels on their way back to Tennessee. Their children weren't allowed to go to school. Veterans finally returning home after the hell they'd been through were attacked and beaten in the streets before they made it home, if they made it home.

Plenty did, and they stubbornly stayed. Their roots were there, most stretching all the way from Germany, Scotland, England, and Ireland. The great-grandparents of those shuffling back from the War of Northern Aggression (yes, many still call it that) brought more than their sun-burned necks with them from the old country. They brought seed, story, and song. Go there today, tomorrow, next week. Buy a bag of vegetables, maybe some flour, cornmeal, or grits and you'll get a story as well, about great-greats crossing the sea with a pocketful of seeds, starting a farm, playing the fiddle while the crops grew, singing songs to pass the time after harvest, songs that still echo across those hills back to the shores of the old country. They will tell you about those same families farming those same fields with seed from those same crops, untouched by the passage of time. The hillbilly – ridiculed, mocked, and derided – has something the rest of us don't. He has memory. He has family. He has tradition tying him to something the tainted gods of progress can never touch. Is that why modernity hates him?

In the Cross-Hairs

There is a much debated document that warrants our attention if only because the nefarious ideas discussed therein are currently in place at various stages in our society. The document is entitled *Silent Weapons for Quiet Wars* and, as the name implies, it details a long-range plan to wage war against the general populace by underhanded and subtle, psychological means. Yes, it initially sounds ridiculous.

And yet, take a moment. Think about the television alone and what its steadily flickering images are called – programs. Think about how much programming the average American is subjected to. Think about the fact that in two short weeks many of those average Americans will be getting into holiday brawls just to save a few bucks on an even bigger programming machine. It's the holiday gift that keeps on giving. Ridiculous? You're damn right it is.

Back to our questionable document. It is roughly forty pages long and "was uncovered quite by accident on July 7, 1986 when an employee of Boeing Aircraft Co. purchased a surplus IBM copier for scrap parts at a sale, and discovered inside" the document in question, or so the story goes. There is, of course, plenty of debate as to its authenticity, but what does it say? What is its purpose? Here is a fine quote that gets straight to the point:

> "It shoots situations instead of bullets; propelled by data processing, instead
> of chemical reaction (explosion); originating from bits of data, instead of grains
> of gunpowder; from a computer, instead of a gun; operated by a computer programmer,
> instead of a marksman; under the orders of a banking magnate, instead of a military
> general…"

Yes, that is exactly what we are experiencing. We are bombarded day and night by propaganda in one form or another. Our personal lives are willingly put on display on this or that social media platform. The banks own us, from the cradle to the grave, or should I say to the slave? Make a slip in your taxes and you will feel the pull of the shackles. Most of us won't dare make that fatal slip. Instead, we'll file all the proper documents by the dates declared. What does *Silent Weapons* have to say about tax day?

> "A good and easily quantified indicator of harvest time is the number of public citizens who pay income tax despite an obvious lack of reciprocal or honest service from the government."

Harvest time? Yes, it actually says that. To assert that we need tax reform may be the understatement of the ages. I love to imagine a furious mob storming the IRS headquarters, but such a thing does not exist in the United States. Why that should be is indeed a valid question, and the report given by the Grace Commission** is a fine place to start on a perilous quest for answers that will take one clear around the globe and back to Puerto Rico, where the brain of the beast resides. Curiouser and curiouser, so they say. That reminds me; our document has something to say about brains,

> "Those who will not use their brains are no better off than those who have no brains, and so this mindless school of jelly-fish, father, mother, son, and daughter, become useful beasts of burden or trainers of the same." *

Admit it. You have thought the same once or twice upon a time, and with good cause. We have, as a whole, allowed ourselves to deteriorate to a tragic-comedic degree. Turn off your televisions. Put down your phones. Disconnect. Read a book, something not assigned in government classrooms. RIGHT NOW. I do not care if you finish this article. Turn it off. This thing we call the internet can be a tool to sharpen our minds, and yet we have generally allowed it to dull our greatest weapon into a rusted and useless heap of near lifeless cells. We are caught in the web. Get out before you are fully ensnared and drained lifeless. Or? Or weave your own web, become active instead of passive. Use the web to expose the spider.

Are you still here? Then I will share another quote from *Silent Weapons*:

> "The general public refuses to improve its own mentality and its faith in its fellow man. It has become a herd of proliferating barbarians, and, so to speak, a blight upon the face of the earth."

Have we? Are we? Sadly, and to a significant degree, the answer is yes. This document is disturbing because it is right. Is it infallible? No. If you took the time to click on this short article then there is life in you yet. Do not concede to their programming. We can each improve our mentality and thus our faith in one another. We can be the barbarians at the gates without being a blight on the earth.

I leave you with one final quote. Take it to heart and never let them tame you.

"No people will tamely surrender their Liberties, nor can any be easily subdued, when knowledge is diffused and virtue is preserved. On the Contrary, when People are universally ignorant, and debauched in their Manners, they will sink under their own weight without the aid of foreign Invaders."

~Samuel Adams

*All quotes from Silent Weapons are taken from the following PDF file:

http://files.meetup.com/196633/SILENT%20WEAPONS%20for%20QUIET%20WARS.pdf

** The Grace Commission Report can be found here and on multiple sites:
http://thetruthnews.info/GraceCommissionReport.pdf

Check, Please!

We have all heard of the absurd notion of "white privilege" and may even have wondered when we could cash our alleged privilege in, but do we know where the idea originated? It was 1988 and Peggy McIntosh published *White Privilege: Unpacking the Invisible Knapsack*, which lists fifty daily effects of "white privilege". Below are enumerated only the ridiculous first five and my responses.

1. *I can, if I wish, arrange to be in the company of people of my race most of the time.*
Well, gee, Peggy, so can anyone else. This is a natural and instinctive separation that happens anywhere, everywhere. It has nothing to do with "whiteness" or "white privilege". Humans naturally segregate. Nature is not politically correct.

2. *I can avoid spending time with people whom I was trained to mistrust and who have learned to mistrust my kind or me.*
No one but life experience "trained" me to mistrust anyone. Of course I will avoid them; one would be stupid not to do so. Why do they mistrust you? Oh, we're back to Nature and She does not care about your feelings or your skin color.

3. *If I should need to move, I can be pretty sure of renting or purchasing housing in an area which I can afford and in which I would want to live.*
Really? Being able to afford a specific location and wanting to live there are two distinct issues; they do not sit hand in hand inside every white person's wallet. I am white, but I do not want to live where I currently do, and yet? Here I sit in the midst of sprawling diversity. I want my privilege check and I want it now. If I get it, I will leave and be accused of white flight. If I move

to a "multi-cultural" neighborhood, I am guilty of gentrification. Put down the pansies! You whites are making your neighbors look bad.

4. *I can be pretty sure that my neighbors in such a location will be neutral or pleasant to me.* Meaning the locations a lot of whites cannot afford? Sure, that is likely. And anywhere else? Most of us ignore our neighbors, whoever they are. Most of us are too busy to really care. I see people of every lazy color stop their car at the mailbox, pull into the driveway and then maybe the garage, and poof! They disappear. I guess that counts as neutral. What about the screaming matches in Ebonics I regularly hear? Is that neutral? It is certainly not pleasant.

5. *I can go shopping alone most of the time, pretty well assured that I will not be followed or harassed.*
We can all choose to shop anywhere we please, whatever color we are. Why would anyone with any sense choose to shop in an area known to be questionable? There are times when I've had no sense and went to a place like Underground Atlanta. Harassed? Yes. Followed? Yes. Clearly, I was not wearing my white privilege shirt. On the flip side, there is a very posh mall here, Phipps Plaza, where I can't afford a single thing though I've stopped once or twice while on a walk just to use their snazzy, marble bathrooms. Who did I see walking hither and thither? Mostly black women…with shopping bags. Well, that's something. Perhaps those who mail out the white privilege checks sent mine to the wrong address.

Clearly, the notion of white privilege is nonsense. There are poor across the color spectrum, just as there are the wealthy and the in-between. If whites are indeed privileged, Ms. McIntosh will need better arguments than this to prove it.

Reparations In Ashes

Imagine if you will a young, black woman driving a shiny, new BMW. Her windows are down and her trite, monotonous tunes are up. Her nails are long and manicured, complete with sparkling bling. Her hair is perfectly straightened and her false eyelashes are bordering on absurd. She is wearing multiple gold chains and enormous hoop earrings along with perfectly matched designer velour lounge-wear. Beside her is an over-sized Louis Vuitton bag with a rhinestone encrusted I-phone laying across the zipper. We've all seen this woman; she's ubiquitous. We'll call her Miss Average.

Imagine another figure, a white woman walking to the store because she does not have a car. Imagine her in discounted work-out wear and worn out shoes. She has no bag, no bling, no manicure. We'll call her Miss Privilege.

Imagine Miss Privilege about to step into the crosswalk because it is her turn, but here comes Miss Average in her BMW, chatting into an earpiece, not looking, pulling into the crosswalk and turning without a care. Imagine Miss Privilege stepping back, out of the way. What did she hear through Miss Average's opened windows? "Bitch better get me my reparations."

Reparations, you say? What, pray tell, does Miss Privilege have to give to Miss Average, or to anyone else? Precious little. Still, the demand is made again and again as this, the Phoenix City, grows ever more divided along race lines. Surely it wasn't like this when Atlanta rose from the ashes of war and rebuilt itself from the ruins. What do those with boots on the ground have to say about it? We have their words still.

It was 1865 and the reconstruction period was brutal. In fact, when one reads the primary sources, one is left asking, reparations from what? There was nothing left. One survivor reports,

> "Desolation met our gaze…abandoned and burned homes, uncultivated land overgrown with bushes; half starved women and children; gaunt, ragged men, stumbling along the road…trying to find their families and wondering if they had a home left."

Do these stumbling, gaunt men owe Miss Average anything? Let's look further. The former planters "went to work doing not what they would but what they could, in the bitter struggle for want with their daily bread." Another Southerner remembered how peculiar it was to see the formerly wealthy "working as a deck-hand on a dirty little river steamer hardly fit to ship cotton on," or "struggling as a porter at a dry good store."

The wealthy planter quite simply had nothing left. And the roughly ninety-five percent of the white population who hadn't been cotton kings? Starving while mourning, barely getting by on "greens, slippery elm bark, and roots." Do they owe Miss Average reparations as well?

Still, places like Atlanta rose from the ashes. What did visitors see in late 1865? A reporter from Boston writes,

> "Every horse and mule and wagon is in active use. The four railroads centering here groan with the freight and passenger traffic, and yet are unable to meet the demand of the nervous and palpitating city. Men rush about the streets with little regard for comfort or pleasure, and yet find the days all too short and too few for the work in hand."

Such were the goings-on of the vanquished. What about the newly freed? What do our eye witnesses have to say about them? I warn you, some of you may be offended, but the witness was there on the streets in 1865 and we were not. What did he say about the freed blacks?

> "They are the most worthless, lazy, thieving set of vagabonds that you can conceive of. They have been turned loose upon us without any idea of making a living for themselves. Their idea of freedom is to have plenty to eat and nothing to do. They flock to the cities, where they get some protection and assistance in stealing from Yankee soldiers."

Such are the contemporaneous accounts of Atlanta immediately after the War. Do not get angry with the writer over the above; it's a quote written by someone who was there. Get mad about this: Atlanta has not changed very much.

*All quotes taken from Thomas Goodrich's *The Day Dixie Died*, a collection of first-hand accounts from the aftermath of the Civil War. This work also includes positive stories, one about a particularly chivalrous freedman named Aleck. He deserves to be remembered, for there are precious few Alecks out there.

White Devils

"History is strewn with the wrecks of nations which have gained a little progressiveness at the cost of a great deal of hard manliness, and have thus prepared themselves for destruction as soon as the movements of the world gave a chance for it."*

I'm going to play the devil's advocate for a moment here. Please bear with me. In defense of young, angry white men who get smeared in every social forum for expressing any sort of white "supremacist" statements, I'd like to assert that they have every right to do so regardless of anyone else's feelings. In fact, they have a duty to defend their race.

Why? Every other race and even trendy social groups du jour, with the glaring exception of heterosexual white males, is allowed to have its faction of angry young men who are sick and tired of being told there's something wrong with them because of their skin color or some other supposedly superficial distinction. Yes, white people are no different. We have a right to be angry as well, particularly when all the woes of the world are placed on our shoulders alone.

It is human nature to blame someone, anyone, when things go wrong. It is likewise human nature to defend oneself. No one should be surprised when a white male fights back; that's exactly what he should do. Yes, anger is a perfectly acceptable reaction to those screeching about universal love and acceptance when these are the same babbling idiots preaching hatred of the white race – Love, love, love… *but we hate this white guy.*

Where is that hatred for the bloodthirsty Bantu who has ravaged more than half of inner Africa? Where is that self-righteous hatred for the marauding bands of rapists who scream to Allah a few times a day? Where is that hatred for the Choctaw who in a fit of rage after losing his black slaves hunted them down like wild animals? It isn't there. The activist hates only the white man; past, present, and future.**

Have we not the right to defend ourselves? Should the white man become a social pariah simply for speaking up for his race as the African or Hispanic man does his? The double standard is perplexing at best. Can we as a species not pause and think for a moment in an attempt to understand why these angry white males are, in fact, angry? If other races can have their screaming young men why shouldn't whites have theirs? This is human nature, plan simple. To expect one race and only that one race to rise above that is – dare I say it – an unconscious admission of that race's superiority.

Whites are expected to behave a certain way, but when angry whites behave like the members of any other angry race the world screams in outrage. To make matters worse, any other race is excused and even coddled in their tantrums. They are labeled as "victims" or their rage is pinned to socio-economic frustration or the racism of – you guessed it – whites. Indeed, when a white expresses any sort of racial frustration, it's incriminating. When any other race does so, it's infinitely excusable. This is some sort of bizarre plot twist in which whites are expected to be better than everyone else. What a conundrum. What a tangled web we weave when we try to lay all the woes of the wide world on a pair of pale shoulders.

Is this the white man's burden? Atlas just shrugged it off and he will not pick up more than his fair share again. If we are truly equals, carry your own burden. Expecting anyone else to do it for you is a confession of inferiority. I urge all of you not to confess to anything but to walk proudly, shouldering your own family, your own tribe, your own race. This is how we all succeed. This is how we all move forward, past the anger.

*http://thinkexist.com/quotation/history_is_strewn_with_the_wrecks_of_nations/327010.html

**Summers, Rachel. *The Forgetting*. Available here: https://www.amazon.com/Forgetting-Mission-Maligned-4/dp/1976412994/ref=asap_bc?ie=UTF8

Just the Facts, Ma'am

Those who control the media, arts, and entertainment on both big screens and small wield a large degree of control over prevailing cultural norms. Those who control the flow of the cultural narrative consequently control to no small degree the prevailing culture itself, and hence its political leanings and general outlook.

Recently, I set out on a cyber quest to find out who exactly is in control of our various screens, and what a quest it has become. Like Percival chasing an elusive Grail or Quixote fighting windmills, I jumped from one site to another with no definitive answers in sight. Any general search undermines the idea of a Jewish controlled media as anti-semitic nonsense and article after self-pitying article pops up about how the Jew is a downtrodden victim of blatant anti-semitism everywhere he or she turns, especially since that dreaded Trump fellow took office.

The Jews have a term for this: Kvetching; that is, whining, moaning, pointing fingers, playing the victim.

I call it the Jericho tactic. Let's make a ruckus over here while another group undermines civilization's walls. No one will notice the shovels and the dynamite over *there* if we wail at this wall over *here* loud enough! Wailing, kvetching, moaning; it's a hell of a distraction tactic. When individuals who ignore the noise march on in a quest for truth lose their jobs and become social pariahs, few will march on. Few will seek the truth. Few will ask questions.

I would like to ask several questions. Why does it feel like chasing one's own tail when doing a simple Google search for a list of CNN executives? Yes, CNN itself has a list, and it is outdated, depending on the search engine used. Google has one list with plenty of former executives. Bing has a completely different list. Why is the information so hard to come by? Why does one get the uneasy feeling that something has been deliberately made elusive while the purveyors of information call it illusive? If the idea that Jews control the media is nothing more than anti-semitic ash, why is it impossible to prove they do not control our screens and print?

The questions are legion and the not-so-kosher answers have seemingly jumped off a cliff, but a trail was left behind. What do we find when we follow it? We find that Ken Jautz, the current President of CNN is Jewish ; he is the executive who fired Rick Sanchez for an anti-semitic rant about Jon Stewart's bigotry and the Jews' disproportionate control of media. Some sites, waiving an obvious bias, say Jauntz is not Jewish. Perhaps he is only a part-time Jew? Whatever the case, this is but one example of internet confusion. The two links below will take you to sites that say he is, in fact, Jewish:
http://www.famousfix.com/topic/ken-jautz/wiki
http://jewprom.50webs.com/JewPromSite_files/sheet107.htm

Moving on to Scot Safon, an executive for Headline News. His name comes up under Google searches for the Jewish film festival, the Jewish music festival, and Jewish Business News. He comes up on a search at the same Jew Prom site listed above, but I can't find his name on the actual list of Jewish broadcasters/entrepreneurs, though he also comes up on an internal search. More confusion and yet, given his obvious involvement in the Jewish community, I'd say he observes Yom Kippur.

Andrew Morse, the Executive Vice President of CNN US and the General Manager of CNN Digital Worldwide is Jewish according to some sites, others don't mention it at all. Nowhere did I see it expressly stated that he was not Jewish. That could (or could not) mean anything. Clearly, concrete information is hard to come by and the verdict is still out.

Many sites are blatantly anti-semitic, and sometimes comedically so, but I am leaving those aside. Below is a paragraph from a site called "Politically Incorrect" that seems to know all of the media's goings-on:

The President of CNN's parent company, Turner Broadcasting, is Jewish (David Levy). His immediate predecessor was also Jewish (Phillip Kent). The majority of Turner's current C-level executives are Jewish. (Doug Shapiro, Lauren Hurvitz, Louise Sims, Howard Shimmel, and several others). CNN's current President is Jewish (Jeff Zucker). Throughout its life, two-thirds

of CNNs' Presidents have been Jewish (Jeff Zucker, Walter Isaacson, Reese Schonfeld, and Burt Reinhardt). CNN's current Vice President is also Jewish (Ken Jauntz). CNN's U.S. Division has had an unbroken stream of Jewish Presidents since at least the mid 1990s. (Ken Jauntz, John Klein, Rick Kaplan, and possibly beyond). The majority of CNN's current Executive VP's are also Jewish. (Allison Gollust, Richard Davis, Amy Entalis, Andrew Morse, and others). Each of the EVP's mentioned in the last sentence were immediately preceded by someone who was also Jewish. (Albie Hecht, Scot Safon, Susan Bunda, and Mark Whitaker, who served as HLN President and CNN EVP, Marketing EVP, Content Development EVP, and Editorial EVP, respectively). Currently, the three highest ranking individuals in CNN's Washington Bureau are Jewish (Sam Feist, Adam Levine, and Eric Sherling).
https://archive.4plebs.org/pol/thread/126317729/

The accuracy of the above is, of course, difficult to determine with any search engine and I do understand why. The question is a sensitive one and I will be the first to admit it is none of my business what religion another person is and quite frankly, I just don't care. The question, however, is not simply one of private religious practice. When an exclusivist people who are a very small percentage of the population control a very large percentage of something as influential as mass media, there are clearly agendas at play that may very well skew any efforts toward objectivity. Just the facts, ma'am? Maybe, or maybe not. And so, the quest continues.

Black and White and Green All Over

As soon as Lincoln was assassinated, countless Yanks swore bloody revenge on the whole of the rebellious South. In one area, all homes were to be draped in black, a landscape in mourning. Rebels who didn't comply were forced, like Mrs. Stuart whose husband and son had both been killed in the war. Mrs. Stuart, you see, didn't want to mourn Lincoln; she felt she'd mourned enough and largely because of him. Occupying soldiers from the North felt differently. They stormed her home, found the black veil she'd used to mourn her husband and son, and forced her to hang it from the front porch. She complied, but only after they agreed to watch her from across the street. She came out a few minutes later in her mourning dress, mounted a chair to hang the veil, and hung it indeed - around her own neck. She swung there, an unforgettable sign of mourning if ever there was one.

Some of you may laugh, shrug it off, or feel she reaped what she sowed. There are some out there who might phrase it more colorfully and say *her ass from Europe…her ass deserve it* as in racially charged online horrors. Anyone who feels this way is the problem. Anyone who feels this way is the reason racism persists. Anyone who feels that one lynching deserves another should be forced to dig the graves, cut down the swollen bodies, and clean up the rancid mess, every last drop. Let them scrub as they listen to a lengthy lecture about the real cause of the war - money. That's right, it wasn't about black and white but about green.

Let me tell you another story about a front porch and a lynching. An old woman, bent and gray, sat on the porch in the master's rocking chair every night, only the war had come and gone and he wasn't the master anymore. He came back from time to time to check on the crops and the old house, but it had fallen to ruin and it didn't seem to matter. He lived in the city now, Savannah maybe. She wasn't sure; that didn't matter either. Nothing did after they killed her boy.

It was all supposed to change when the Yanks came. They called it freedom, but what did that mean? The freedom to starve? She stayed where she was with her daughters and a few others. Together, they worked the land, tried to take care of what was left of the house but only the rodents and birds nesting in its once elegant parlors appreciated her efforts. Still, it felt like her house now, even the scorch marks and bullet holes, so she swept and scrubbed like she'd always done. All the white folks were gone, coming back occasionally to collect their monthly dues and remind her it wasn't hers after all. Still, they grew enough food and kept a solid roof over their heads. That was more than a lot of free folk could say.

She and her daughters even had new dresses; they'd hid some of the master's valuables when the Yanks came and never told him about the silver in the back yard. No, they sold it and spent the money on necessities, knowing God would understand. The Yanks took everything else to pay for the war, of course. They said it was a war for her, to win her freedom, but she didn't believe that anymore. Her boy went North to go to school and he told her the war was about something called politics and the Union, said the North just needed the South for money and the dead President had got on the wrong side of the banks. She didn't know what that meant, but she trusted her boy; he could read.

Her other boy was dead, but she thought about him every night on that front porch. It was around that same time of night when they rode through on stomping horses, the one in front carrying a coiled rope. He did it, they said. He was the nigger who raped the white girl. *What white girl? There ain't no white girls 'round here.* Followed by, *Don't lie to me, boy.* And that was all the trial he got. She found him the next day, dangling in the woods behind the house. He was dead and her other boy was gone, though he did visit once or twice. There were no jobs here for a more or less educated black man, so he had to leave. She missed him, but she was proud of him. He wrote to her often, forgetting perhaps that she couldn't read. Still, she kept all his letters in a trunk at the foot of her sunken bed, every single one of them.

Rocking on that front porch, she remembered her boys. She remembered the war; it still didn't seem real, and neither did freedom though she had a piece of paper that said she was free. She couldn't read it, of course, but it was important and so she kept inside the trunk with her boy's letters. No, it didn't seem real even as she sat in the master's chair night after night. Maybe it would feel real if she left the old house, but where would she go? What would she eat? There was too much possibility, good and bad. Was that freedom? She was content to stay where there was a roof and a meal, knowing she could walk away if she chose to do so. That was freedom enough.

The rocker kept groaning and her mind kept wandering. Her daughter was pregnant; was it the master's? Probably. He kept less of the dues when she was 'nice' to him. Maybe the baby would have his blue eyes. She hoped so; her son had those eyes, but it was hard to tell the way they bulged over that rope. She knew those men could see his cloudy blue eyes, begging for mercy before they shoved a rope over his head. They knew he was the master's son and they didn't care. Maybe that's why he grabbed the white girl, if there was one. Maybe he wanted to avenge his mother and sister by taking one of theirs, if that's what happened.

If so, he was foolish, even cruel. Why add fuel to a fire that was already dwindling away? She hoped folks would stop being so cruel to each other; it was only a decade or so since the war, after all. There was hope. She didn't know Mrs. Stuart and the countless others who'd given up all hope ten years ago. Instead, she rocked on the front porch until the old chair moved slower and slower then creaked to a stop. This was her last night on the front porch; they found her the next morning still in her favorite chair, cold. They used the wood from the chair and the front porch to make her coffin. She would have wanted it that way.

I like to think Mrs. Stuart and the old woman are on a porch somewhere together, shaking their heads at our continued stupidity. If you knew they were watching, what would you do? Would you act differently towards one another? Their memory alone should suffice; their stories enough to warrant at least decency. So many stories, so many perspectives and yet somehow, with time and a politically advantageous narrative, our memories become simplified, watered-down, dumbed-down into villains and victims, white and black, axis and allies. Nothing is ever so simple.

*Excerpted from *The Forgetting* by Rachel Summers. Release date September 22, 2017. The story of Mrs. Stuart is factual, the rest is fiction based on primary source material.

Poetry and Patriotism

The blonde beast was yawning, stretching, rubbing his tired eyes. A clamor in the distance snapped him to attention. Chants of hatred coming from those who claim to promote love. The erasure of culture by those who promote the multi-cult. Acts of violence committed by those who scream for peace. It was clamor enough to awaken the gods, and well it may if the noise continues. Something else, however, was awakened that fine, summer day in the Old South. Charlottesville, Virginia made such a noise that the collective soul of a drowsy people was forced from slumber. *Kill whitey*, some of them screamed while the others marched on, their footsteps echoing deep into the layers of history buried under the city's concrete. What did the ancestors hear?

It was not part of their blood,
It came to them very late,
With long arrears to make good,
When the Saxon began to hate.

They were not easily moved,
They were icy — willing to wait
Till every count should be proved,
Ere the Saxon began to hate.

Their voices were even and low.
Their eyes were level and straight.
There was neither sign nor show
When the Saxon began to hate.

It was not preached to the crowd.
It was not taught by the state.
No man spoke it aloud
When the Saxon began to hate.

It was not suddenly bred.
It will not swiftly abate.
Through the chilled years ahead,
When Time shall count from the date
That the Saxon began to hate.

~Rudyard Kipling

I recited the *Wrath of the Awakened Saxon* in my mind as I marched through the turbulent streets of Charlottesville that day. I felt it; something had awakened. I wondered as I dodged insults and rocks, what rough beast slouches toward Charlottesville to be born? His name is Saxon, Teuton, Viking, Celt. His name is Conquistador, Roman, Spartan. His name is Western Civilization and he will not be lulled to sleep again.

Crosswalk Sleepwalk

It happens at least once every week. I approach an urban crosswalk in the early morning. There are no cars in sight. There is one person, maybe two, standing on the corner waiting for the light to change and give the walk signal. Again, there are no cars in sight, so I walk on with no regard for the lights, pass the frozen pedestrians, and cross the street. When they see this, they seem startled for a few seconds, then they predictably follow me. I know now; if you walk, the sleepwalkers will follow. It happens regularly enough that I have noticed and pondered this strange phenomenon. Why would anyone stand and wait for permission from an unseen force when permission is not needed? Why wait on nothing? Perhaps some souls wait for permission because they need to be told what to do. Perhaps their kind will wait in a stupor until there is no one left to give orders. Perhaps these souls have been waiting since 1984.

There are other inexplicable crosswalk phenomena. At a busy intersection in Atlanta, there is a crosswalk going to the park. There is no light, just polite and ineffective signs reminding drivers to stop for walkers. They rarely do, and so the walkers pile up on the sidewalk waiting for a chance to cross. They would wait until they turned gray if not for one intrepid soul who simply walks around the crowd, puts out her hands, steps into the crosswalk, and crosses the busy street…with a herd of walkers fast on her heels. Sometimes this brave walker angrily knocks on the crosswalk sign. Once, she picked up a caution cone and threw it into the crosswalk. Of course, it is not always so dramatic. One way or another, the cars will stop. They will stop when a walker asserts herself and then the crowd can cross. They will not stop, however, if one stands blankly on the sidewalk and stares longingly at the park on the other side. In short, the citizen must DO something.

Sometimes, after a crosswalk tantrum, I think of the simple act of crossing a road as a microcosm of our assertion to our rights. Sure, we as American citizens have this beautifully written document detailing our rights, and yet we should never expect them to simply be handed to us. We should never expect that any unseen force will care. We should never expect others going about the business of their rights to care about ours. Sometimes, while walking through this life, we have to take what is ours. These our are rights. We can take them. We can act on them. We can live by them. We need not wait for permission. We need not wait passively for someone to give us our turn. Take it. DO something.

It happened again just this morning. I approached a crosswalk. The lights were out, blinking at each other across the void. A man stood there waiting for nothing. Waiting on no cars. Waiting on lights that were not even working. I walked around him, into the crosswalk, and across the street. It was that simple. Before I made it across, I was listening behind me. I was on the fifth painted bar when it happened – he followed me across. I knew he would; they always do. Why? There was no reason to stand there. There was no reason to wait. He could have crossed that road anytime. He could have taken his right.

Citizens, what are you waiting for? Your rights are waiting.

Never the Norse

The masses are rootless, severed from their ancestral sources and told we are all one - and this from the same venom-dripping tongues that preach the values of the multi-cult. Multi, that is, unless you are of Norse descent and hold to Asatru. Of African descent? Then embrace your Orishas! Of Arabic descent? Let us make concessions for your Islam. Of Celtic descent? Let us scream racist and tear your culture from you the second you start to remember. Teutonic? How dare you bring up anything that stinks of Germanicism. This will get you blacklisted, fired, or at the least protested.

Such is the case with author Bryan Wilton, a prolific writer on the Nordic and Germanic religious traditions. Recently, at an independent bookstore in Atlanta, Georgia, it was proposed that he do a book signing. The owner shot down the idea immediately. Why? Norse mythology!? He might be a white supremacist. He was deemed a risk at roughly the same time that the African religions section was doubled, and subsequently plundered.

Mr. Wilton is hosting a book signing and discussion, however, and he has hosted many. His next event will be on August 19th [2017] at Mojo Mama's in Independence, Missouri - and what an unnecessary uproar it has caused. Antifa has decided that the author is a threat to the left-wing agenda and they are protesting the event and promising trouble. They have harassed the store owner and generally made fools of themselves - may they push Mr. Wilton's book sales through the proverbial roof. Just the same, Mr. Wilton, an infantry veteran who served for seven years, promises that his freedom of speech will not be inhibited, nor should it be. If you are in Independence on the nineteenth of August, stop by and show some support. If we are at the point where book signings are considered a threat, we are at a low point indeed.

That bookstore in Atlanta hit a low point when Mr. Wilton was refused. Sadly, their refusal isn't surprising; there any non-white tradition is catered to, for such fosters the appearance of magnanimity, compassion, and progressive open-mindedness. What isn't so apparent are dollar-store candles hastily labeled with this or that charm, priced at ten times their worth, and sold to the credulous - and it isn't just candles. Snake oil for sale, marketed to the darker masses, and all under cover of enlightened acceptance. Why? Because they will buy whatever you tell them to buy. To some touting the multi-cult's horn, green is the only color that matters.

What matters to followers of Asatru is the preservation and practice of tradition without any infringement on freedom of religion. Perhaps our protesters should be reminded that we do have that freedom. What matters to any patriot is the preservation and practice of our freedom of speech. Perhaps our protesters should be reminded of that as well. Finally, what matters to those worth a damn is genuine diversity, a diversity that includes those of Norse and Teutonic descent. Embrace your Northern roots, cast your runes, and remind any nay-sayers that a rainbow is only white light, broken into lesser pieces.

The Trap

Imagine this: You've lost a war. You've lost your fortune and maybe even your home, but you still have land and on that land is a fine crop of cotton. With this harvest you can rebuild something of your former life. Sure, you have to pay the field hands, but you're not feeding, clothing, or sheltering them any more so the difference shouldn't take too much of your profits. In fact, you will likely make more money as chattel slavery is an impractical, costly, and outmoded form of labor. Slaves were being freed slowly but surely before the war; yours were long gone before that fateful first shot. War or no war, hiring labor was a better prospect and it was almost time for a harvest.

Here come the Cottentots, Yankees who convinced the newly freed slaves that stealing was acceptable. So, your workers stole your harvest and sold it for next to nothing to the intruding Cottentot who then sold it again, likely to another Yankee, for a substantial mark-up. You're left with nothing but a claim that will never be addressed by law enforcement that is no longer local but imposed by your conquerors from the North. No one who cares has any authority here.

And on the other side of town? A school for freed slave children where Yankee teachers instill in those young minds ideas of innate equality but an unfair balance of power - the white man has the power, they whisper, only because of the money they have and they stole that money from the fruits of African labor. It was during the so-called Reconstruction that an irreparable racial divide was born that one disgruntled North Carolinian felt would ripen into a harvest of blood and murder.

Are your scythes raised? What will you bring in from the fields? While the harvest may be uncertain, it seems that the powers-that-be, whomever they be, want us to hate one another. With a consistently infantilized, dumbed-down, and agitated population that is not hard to do. Like that pink house getting so much attention in Atlanta, it's a trap. Will you fall for it?

Far too many will. Why do the string pullers want us to hate one another? It's a question with myriad possible answers and the right one is likely under a pile of ill-gotten wealth in the vault of an offshore bank. This is the accumulation of an ongoing effort to break down the human spirit, to arrest our development, and to demoralize us – all of us – to the point that society crumbles. One post-war Alabamian summed it up nicely when he said,

> "We have just emerged from the ruins of the most gigantic and terrible war recorded in history. And while we have spilled the best blood of our land, and lost our liberties and property, who can say that we have escaped the next greatest calamity of war ~ the demoralization of society."

And on march the destroyers. Why? What is to be gained from the breakdown of civilization as we know it? It's simple, really. Solve et Coagula. Those who destroy will be those who rebuild, according to their own specifications. While our society has its rotten places that should be demolished and rebuilt, we needn't demolish our relationships with each other. Instead, these should be fortified and protected against those who would scream racism at every turn. Don't get caught in the trap.

Beyond Vietnam: A Veteran's Recollections

Many called it the war that shouldn't be, but it was a war just the same and it divided this country like no war ever had. Far too many of our soldiers never made it home. Those who did have tales to tell. One such soldier recently spoke to me about his experiences in Vietnam and beyond. He had been in the Navy for twenty-two years, climbed to the rank of Chief in less than eleven years, and among other things, is now a retired classified weapons expert. The short version: he built the bombs that rained down on Vietnamese jungles and then some.

I asked him about the infamous Gulf of Tonkin incident. The theory on countless YouTube channels is that this attack was a false flag, that the Tonkin Gulf Resolution was drafted before the attack happened, that there were no Vietnamese torpedo boats. How did the Chief feel about this? He scoffed,

> "No one spends that much money and effort just to fake something; but it wasn't the Vietnamese…"

The Chief told me that the Chinese had been in North Vietnam causing trouble. He stated unequivocally that it was they who sent two planes after US ships. I had never heard that, but one does not argue with the Chief. We moved on to current affairs. Antifa? Social Justice Warriors? Black Lives Matter? His response:

> "This country was built on fundamental concepts. If you disagree with those concepts, you should find somewhere else to live. Every bleeding heart liberal needs to go to a foreign country and experience a police state. They'd change

their minds."

What about the very touchy issue of Muslim immigration? His answer was so simple and so direct, a liberal's head might spin,

> "No one should be allowed into this country whose people have openly expressed the desire to kill us and our way of life."

Yes, it is that simple. Still, here were are, divided again, forty-two years after Vietnam's official end and we are still screaming at each other. We treated our troops poorly when they got home, as if they wanted to be shipped off to a foreign jungle only to crawl through the mud and blood while getting shot at and watching their friends blown to bits. This was around the time our so-called journalists started playing people against each other, initially the working class and the hippies. They conveniently forgot the government's role. Average Americans were spitting on each other. And why?

The why of it all is hard to nail down. Whatever the case, war is a money making racket reserved for the elite few who invest in it. And you had better believe those who risk their cash are not risking their lives. To blame some poor kid who could not avoid the draft rather than blaming the corrupt system that sent him to war is to miss the point entirely. I am willing to bet the average soldier did not want the war any more than the average hippie did.

As for the Chief, he was not drafted. He was sworn in on his eighteenth birthday, in 1969, and was sent to those murky Vietnamese waters in 1970. He was there for roughly three years. We can learn more from him than from any textbook and he is not the only one with tales to tell. Listen to our veterans and our elders. Tell their stories; for this is how history comes to life and carries on.

Reputable charities for US Veterans:
http://www.shepherdsmen.com/
http://www.nmcrs.org/

Then They Came for Another Piece

The news was all over town, all over the region. Someone declared the Confederate statues offensive. Someone said Take 'Em Down, and so they did. Protestors were assuaged with promises of a museum. Still, we were angry, but the mayor said it had to be this way. They dismantled our past and hauled it away. It was going to a museum, so it would be safe, right? We watched and shrugged; it's just a few statues.

Then they came for another piece.

We went to the museums to see what we could no longer see, but something was missing. Someone declared the Confederate flag offensive. Someone said Take 'Em Down, and so they did. Now there is an empty flag pole, blank spaces on the walls. Emptiness. They promised things would be safe in a museum; we cringed and paid the admission price. They took it down anyway. We watched and shrugged; it's just a flag.

Then they came for another piece.

Monuments to the Confederate dead are surely safe. Still, someone has declared the obelisk a reminder of painful things. We offer a monument of their own, and they scoff. Someone will say Take 'Em Down, and so they will, piece by piece. They call it progress, moving forward, reparations for historical wrongs. We argue and we are shut down as racist, backward, bigots. We watch and shrug; it's just a monument.

Then they will come for another piece.

Where will it end? With the dead themselves? I've heard it mentioned. What about our children's textbooks, surely there is something offensive in there. What about the street signs? Take 'Em Down, someone will shriek. And so they will disappear, one piece at a time. Will the erasers then move Northward? Will the Yankee at last understand the South's lament when Boston's Freedom Trail is declared offensive and paved over? Such a rebellious attitude is best forgotten. Will the erasers then move Westward, striking down anything reminiscent of cowboys and outlaws? Such a rebellious attitude is best forgotten. Why stop there? Rebels are everywhere in this land of the free, not just in the South. They will come for another piece, and it may be in your back yard.

The time to take a stand is now, not tomorrow. Not next week. Now. Get to know your local history. Call your congressmen. Contact your local historic preservation groups. Go to your local schools and tell stories about what happened on the ground where that building now stands. History is everywhere. Learn it. Feel it. Share it. Don't let them come for yet another piece.

http://www.npr.org/2017/05/20/529232823/with-lee-statues-removal-another-battle-of-new-orleans-comes-to-a-close
http://www.ajc.com/news/local/with-confederate-flags-gone-civil-war-museum-will-close/ogScTPPdqliC0z4opJ3GTI

The Forgetting:

A Creeping Death

Monuments are being removed. Why? The powers-that-be want you to forget. They want us all uprooted, with nothing to cling to, nothing to fight for. Those without tradition make for a malleable population, you see. That is simply not good enough. In fact, it's inexcusable. So is the average American's poor knowledge of the Civil War, otherwise known as the War Between the States, or the War of Northern Aggression. Ask any passerby, why did it happen? Most will respond with an automatic, *because of slavery*. Let it be known that this damn war was not about slavery or human rights at all. This bloodbath on our soil was not about black or white. The Civil War, like most wars, was about money and power.

States had a Constitutional right to secede should the Federal government overstep its bounds, and overstep it did in the form of costly tariffs on cotton goods imported from Europe. The result? European buyers, being fleeced by the North, offered less money for raw cotton in the South. Consider the so-called Tariff of Abomination of 1828, which raised the tariff on imported cotton products to one-third their selling price. Due to public outcry, this was lowered but more increases were threatened. When Lincoln was elected in 1860, the South know full well its markets could not absorb the cost of another tariff.

With laws and tariffs being imposed from the North, the South exercised their right to secede. The Attorney General at the time ruled that it was indeed their right and that the Federal government could lawfully do nothing about it; unless the seceding states started a war, that is. Enter the drama at Fort Sumter. Lincoln insisted on sending provisions to a "starving" garrison but what he sent were war provisions. Sumter's garrison was not starving; we have correspondences between those within and without the fort pertaining to grocery deliveries. In fact, relations between the garrison and the town were peaceful if not amicable, until armed reinforcements arrived. It was then that the South fired the first shot and they took the fort before it could be filled with hostile troops. The garrison was allowed to leave peacefully. Not a single Union soldier was harmed.

The outcome, nonetheless, was war. Even with the above information in hand, some will argue that slavery was a reason. Was it? Here's some more information: There were plenty of abolitionists in the South, whereas plenty of Northerners wanted to retain the status quo because, well, those rowdy slaves might move into *their* neighborhoods. In 1750, both Virginia and South Carolina passed anti-slavery laws. England nullified these laws. By the dawn of the nineteenth century it was far more profitable to hire wage workers than to buy and maintain slaves. In short, slavery was a dying institution; war was not necessary to bring it to an end. In the first decade of the 1800's, legislation was introduced from Georgia to abolish slavery and reimburse the owners to encourage them to free their property. It was voted down by non slave-holding states.

Let's look briefly now at the Great Emancipator, Abe Lincoln. When the war had been burning for more than a year, he refused to take any action to free the slaves. The Emancipation Proclamation came a year later, and only affected states and areas still under Confederate control. The idea, you see, was to create chaos and thereby give the Union every advantage. Further, this put the South at a moral disadvantage - it seemed they were now fighting to preserve slavery. So how did Southerner's feel about slavery? Some surely wanted to keep their slaves, but these were in a shrinking minority. Others, like Robert E. Lee himself, said that slavery "was a moral and political evil." He further asserted that the "best men of the South" oppose it. Guess who's statue is next on NOLA's chopping block? The statue of General Robert E. Lee, an opponent to slavery.

Obviously, the Civil War was not simply a black and white issue. Nonetheless, those who would erase our past want you to think it is. Why? If you protest the removal of history, you must be a racist. This shuts down opposition and those wielding the cultural erasers can do as they please. To those who scream racist at every turn: At this point, the word racist has lost all meaning. Call me what you will. I hereby protest.

For further reading, see John S. Tilley's short introduction on the matter entitled, *Facts the Historians Leave Out: A Confederate Primer*. A more in-depth treatment of the war and its aftermath can be found in Thomas Goodrich's *The Day Dixie Died*, a book rich in primary source material. Primary sources are invaluable, for if you don't believe me, you will find it hard to argue with those who lived through it.

Don't Take Candy From Strangers

There was once a witch in the wood who snared young men with candies that made them feel real good, and they couldn't get enough. They wanted more and more of the candy; it became their weakness and so the witch was able to lock them in cages and fatten these young men for the inevitable slaughter. This clever and hungry witch is reminiscent of our corrupt government which has offered illicit candies to countless young men, then locked them up to fatten them for a coming slaughter. The question is, whose slaughter? Further, what happens to them in their cages?

We all know that inner-city neighborhoods were deliberately flooded with drugs and the result was arrest and imprisonment for the thousands who couldn't just say no. A lot happens in a prison; some find faith. It is estimated that one in three black prisoners converts to Islam. While they are being actively indoctrinated - recruited we might say - they are also being taught how to be better criminals; this is what prison does. In other words, our prison system is a potential terrorist breeding ground. I say potential only because, like it or not, Islam provides genuine conversion to some of these young men who need to put down the liquor and drugs. Islam helps them do this.*

It does much more to some converts. It teaches them to use religion to manipulate the government into giving them special treatment. It teaches them to hate white America. It teaches them victimhood and the need for vengeance. What happens when these prisoners are released? More crime is likely, which leads to more laws and bigger government; this we all see. What we don't see is this: Yet another wedge is driven between the black and white communities.

Divide and Conquer works. With the masses squabbling amongst themselves, the government grows as if feeding on our hatred, animosity, and pain - all of which is misdirected. Whatever color we are and whatever part of town we're from, WE HAVE THE SAME ENEMY. He is not at our side, he is above us, pulling our strings, emptying our wallets, and telling us to embrace diversity even as he stirs and prods our inherent prejudices. Wedge after wedge is driven in.

Those in cages who are fattened on a religion that encourages racism are especially susceptible to this. Are they being fattened for their own slaughter or ours? Frankly, I don't think our government cares as long as we continue killing one another. The witch will eat her fill regardless. There is, of course, a way out of this nightmarish tale for we are not just characters but writers.

We can refuse the candies, whether we find them in tiny bags behind the corner market, in neatly labeled bottles at the (p)harmacy, or in the constant bombardment of images from the telescreens. We can choose to fatten ourselves from the fruits of our own gardens. We can write ourselves out of the cages, cut our strings, and walk off the stage. We can let the witch starve.

* *Building Radical Islam in America: Part One.* See the following: http://crazzfiles.com/building-radical-islam-in-america-part-1/

The Beginning of the End:

One Apocalypse and a Culture to Go, Please

Nietzsche's Zarathustra warned us, "The good have always been the beginning of the end," but it seems the message was lost somewhere in the shuffle of anti-German propaganda. Just the same, we know it to be true even as we passively watch the good tell us we must integrate, tolerate, and beg forgiveness. We also know that the end is merely a new beginning. Is this what we long for, a chance to rise from the ashes just to see if we can do it? Is this the end game of the West's so-called Faustian soul?

Der Wille zur Macht, he called it. The Will to Power; it is this which drives man forward, particularly Western European man, but will it drive him forward off a cliff? Perhaps. Originally, we moved forward toward external mastery, then master over one's self became the goal. This ambition, like most, can only be realized through the control of instinctual impulses, delayed gratification, and knowledge of self. Here I posit an idea: has Western man created this crisis with Islam as an external manifestation of his last battle with himself? Did we need something so Other against which to firmly define ourselves? Is the refugee merely a monster that we must first release and then defeat, like some goaded beast once locked away in the bowels of our collective Coliseum? The beasts' handlers, the social justice brigade and their kind, want us to lose and they have trained their beasts well; 'tis a dangerous game we play.

If the refugee is Western man's last frontier made manifest, whence begins the conquest? When we realize that what we are doing is not a game. Our conscious selves have forgotten our own philosophies, forgotten that self-actualization comes to us via hardship; but our souls remember and so we've opened our borders and invited hardship to live with us. When Zarathustra spoke he said, "I am that which must overcome itself again and again." Is that what we are doing now? Did we in the West grow so complacent without significant challenge that we created challenge to the point of suicide?

Prometheus Unbound missed his tethers; he needed a challenge and quite frankly, modernity with all its ease, is boring. Everything has become far too civilized, except the refugee. Here is a beast roaming and stalking; another example of the perennial conflict between barbarity and civility, between being and becoming.** Western man is bored with being and desires to become again. It is curious but possible that we have invited beasts to live among us in hopes of awakening and releasing the slumbering beast within ourselves. Are we looking to the only barbarians we can find to challenge us, to wake us finally from our complacency and decadence?

If so, the refugee crisis is a subconsciously requested wake-up call, only thousands upon thousands of us are still asleep while the beast roams. This will not do. Wake up! Face the challenges so brashly created. In overcoming, we will become again and this is what Western man needs. This decline of the West, what many call an apocalypse, is just that – a lifting of the veil, for that is what the word means. What do we see when it is lifted? We see that this ending is but a new beginning. Wake up. Grab your swords. Start the world.

* Nietzsche, Friedrich. *Thus Spoke Zarathustra*. There are countless editions of this book. Read it!
** This idea was promoted in the writings of the historian William McNeill, who is know for his works on Western Civilization. McNeill was a professor at the University of Chicago. He died less than one year ago.

Whether with Pen or Sword

Freedom of the Press. Freedom of Speech. We call these things freedom, but are we truly free? It was once said that if you want to find out who is in power, all you need do is find out who you're not allowed to criticize. Of course, you can say it, write it, publish it anyway, but you may lose your job. Your dissertation proposal will not be approved. You will never find a mainstream publisher. In some countries, you may go to jail.

Using your freedoms is then tantamount to social if not professional suicide, or worse; and so, many would-be dissenters and truth-tellers bow down then fall in line. This is not freedom. This is manipulation at best, intellectual tyranny at worst. Why must our language be so tightly controlled? Words are powerful weapons, powder kegs of thought capable of igniting revolution should the right voice at the right time utter the right combination. With spelling, you see, a spell is cast!

Historically, gunpowder and printing blazed across Europe together. This is no coincidence. Both are manifestations of ingenious distance tactics. Why engage sword to chest when you can hurl bombs or leaflets? The one tears at the flesh, the other at the spirit. Both are effective weapons. The Reformation was the first conflict to see flyers and field guns. The French Revolution was the first to see mass distribution of pamphlets and mass-fire artillery. The fire-bombing of words, words, words against Napoleon taught the truth-spinners something - a certain turn of phrase can be used to control the thought processes of the reader.

Writers who challenge the current propaganda are done away with, one way or another, while readers have only illusory choices in what they read. Again, this is not freedom. How, then, does one get at the truth? If the truth is merely that which is expounded by the press for a few weeks until a fluid tale is solidified, one can get at the truth anywhere. If the truth is, in fact, the truth, then finding it is decidedly more problematic. Speaking or printing it? Go ahead and prepare the noose.

Because such seekers and speakers are few and far between, the truth-spinners march on, doling out a pre-approved narrative that fits the agenda of the day. The mass of readers and listeners simply believe, brush aside, or even ridicule in a meme or two. Still, no formal challenge is made. No gauntlet is thrown. And so, the accepted narrative stands.

What does this narrative do to the masses? It enslaves them, like trained beasts. When that newspaper hits the sidewalk, when the morning news flickers on, when the internet is bombarded - Pavlov may as well ring his bell. The targeted masses salivate; they may even take to the streets and have a protest or two. Manipulated, they may turn on each other. Yet again, this is not freedom. This is performance and the truth-spinners have tied us up in their threads as they pull this way and that.

Pull back! Pull them from behind the curtain and tear down the stage! Fight fire with fire, words with words. Be the shield, that hardened point where the spell of the spellers is returned to the source so that its poison can no longer affect those who stand behind you; and that crowd will grow, for the truth finds its own way in the world and just one taste of it creates a life-long addict.

The truth-spinners and their pre-approved narratives have never tasted so good. Every ending is a new beginning. As the tales of the truth-spinners unravel - and unravel they will - take those threads and weave anew the fabric of the universe. Turn their words upside down and shake out the truth. One by one, the manipulated masses will sniff it out, but know this: in the beginning, you will not attract the trained dog but the wolf, he or she who was never truly a member of the domesticated pack. This is the freethinker, the barbarian at the gates. As this civilization crumbles, as one word at a time jabs and pricks at their faulty armor, we will break through. Countless dogs will turn on their masters and join us. Together, we will run over the ruins and start the world anew. This, finally, is freedom.

Ubiquitous Fascism:

Or How to Make a Word Meaningless

Oh, fascism! Perhaps the most incorrectly and overused word of recent months. He's a fascist! You're a fascist! This is a fascist bill! This is a fascist ideology! and on and on we drone, slapping labels on everyone and everything with whom we disagree. It's only fascist, of course, when the other guy is doing it, whatever it is. While the government has drawn imaginary lines in quickly shifting sands, it pretends to fight itself and the vast majority of Americans are heartily entertained by these suit and tie gladiators hurling empty words at one another across various media outlets, outlets that are more often than not in the pockets of the very politicians they pretend to report. And the independents? Let's call them terrorists. That ought to shut them up.

And those labeled fascist? Today they are legion. Is the label, or libel, accurate? No. Then what is a fascist? The definitions vary, of course. Historically, fascism arose from a war-torn landscape. Desperate times call for desperate measures, and so a dictator is born. A fascist dictator is meant to hold absolute power over his subjects and his country, pulling both from a crisis situation. Any who disagree with his methods or oppose him are silenced. By this generic definition, no one in American politics today rightly qualifies as an outright fascist. Many, possibly most, may have fascist leanings (read hero complex and/or power trip) but such may be a necessary character trait for anyone mad enough to step into a political ring in the first place. Is this a condemnation? No. A certain personality is required for an on-the-stage leader and they may well all have a dose of fascism running through their veins. Such is the nature of the beast.

Then why all the name calling? Imagine if you will the politician of your choice staring intently into a mirror. His opponent approaches from the other side and so he points around the mirror and calls him or her the last thing he saw in his own reflection – that which he buries deeply, that which he knows will frighten his constituents. Accurate or not, the masses hate the word and any who bear its mark.

Let's take one of these anonymous masses and drop him pint-sized onto a bookshelf. Over the years he's wandered the oddly prophetic pages of Nietzsche, Rand, and Bradbury's book burnings. Now he's hopped straight into Orwell's *1984*. Ah, now here is fascism! Here is a distorted reflection of current trends, enough to frighten anyone with eyes to see and ears to hear. Out with the books! Out with freethinking! In with floods of mind-numbing technology, diluted language, and illusory class divisions! Just do your job. Just keep your head down and wear a false smile. Everything will be fine. Let the government take care of you.

What does that sound like? US. Perhaps we are the true fascists, the ones who went along with it all, bit by constricting bit. Dictators, after all, are not just born amidst the rubble and ashes of war. They are born amidst the crushed hopes and dreams of a people who no longer want to think or do for themselves. Dictators are created by those whom they rule. So scream *fascist* if you will. Just remember that you, too, were looking in a mirror but a moment ago.

The Color of History

I recently interviewed a former high school history teacher who taught at a public school in North Georgia. He was kind enough to tell me about his teaching experiences as well as his family history. I will call him Mr. Brown, as he wishes to remain anonymous.

Mr. Brown and I went to college together many years ago and we have been friends since those memorable days, both sharing a love for history and a passion for truth. He's told me many stories about his frustrations as an educator, but he enjoyed the experience nonetheless. Clearly, teaching is a mixed bag, as with anything. Mr. Brown, however, has a unique perspective. He is a predominately African-American male who is also what we might call a Civil War buff. His students may have expected the go-to narrative wherein the war is blamed on slavery, but, to Mr. Brown's credit, he gave his students a more balanced version of events. Here is what he said on the subject:

> "I taught the Civil war very much as white teachers had taught it to me. I taught that slavery, particularly the extension thereof was a central factor of what happened during

the Civil War. But I also taught that it wasn't the only factor. There was also the friction from sectionalism, the deaths of men like Stephen Douglas, Daniel Webster, and Henry Clay, the emergency of the Republican party…etc. The Civil War didn't occur in a slavery vacuum, and that's what I tried to impress on my students."

Mr. Brown also has a unique perspective on the so-called black experience, for his family has a unique history. I remember the day he told me that not all blacks were slaves, that some black families even owned slaves themselves. He suspected his family was such a family. Why? They weren't like the other families; they had money. How did they get it?

"There were always whispers and rumors about how my grandmother's family
came by it's land and money. Whenever we'd talk about history my grandmother
would urge me to remember that black people owned slaves as well, I asked her,
before she died, if our family owned slaves. She said that we don't talk about that,
and we never did again. What I do know is that my great- great-grandfather rode
around in a buggy loaning money to blacks and whites. My great-grandfather owned
a huge part of the county that they lived in and he sent all of his children to college.
They had a large amount of money, property, and power at a time when most blacks
were sharecropping. Were they slave owners? I don't know, but they were doing
something…"

Of course, the next logical question is this: Was your family always free?

"I don't know if my family was always free in this country. My great-great-
grandfather on my father's mother's side appears in the 1870 census. That's as
far back as that part of my family goes. There's a Bible with the names and dates
of the people born in that part of the family going back to almost when they came
here in the 1700's, but it's so old that the ink has run… It was always said that at
least by the outbreak of the Civil War, my dad's mother's people were free and thriving."

What are my conclusions? History is infinitely more complicated than we have been told. To pretend anything about the American South is as plain as black and white is a gross oversimplification. When the latest Hollywood release or the newest political bandwagon tells you otherwise, question the narrative. When another Confederate statue is thrown down the memory hole, think about Mr. Brown's surprising family and the lessons they hold for us all. Think of the white indentured servants whose necks were red from working the fields while their cracker families cracked corn because there was nothing else to eat. No, history is never as simple as black and white.

Franken-Fury

Sometimes experiments go horribly awry. Sometimes dogs turn on their masters. Sometimes puppeteers get tangled in their own strings and fall from the rafters. We may have seen a brief foreshadowing of this at the now notorious Evergreen State, the site of mob protests, anti-white non-sense, and generally thuggish behavior. Evergreen is a generously, liberally (and publicly) funded college in Washington with roughly twenty-nine percent various non-white students. These minority students took over the campus on a planned "Day of Absence" at which no whites were supposed to attend, neither students nor professors.

One professor, Bret Weinstein – a Jewish, leftist, liberal by his own account – spoke out against this day as blatantly racist. This is significant because by and large, protest groups on our college campuses have been encouraged or even created by professors who identify just as Weinstein does. They created a monster and this monster visited Weinstein's classroom on the so-called Day of Absence. The monster didn't care how this professor identified; they saw a white male and decided he wasn't supposed to be there. There was a confrontation, of course, and the president of the school ultimately sided with the monster.

Weinstein soon discovered that those most concerned with defending him and his rights to free speech were not his allies on the left, but the anathema of campus – the right wingers. Did he have a change of heart after this incident? Maybe. Will other professors think twice before encouraging the monster? Maybe not. Some may drag it along until the leash breaks and then? They may try to cater to the monster's demands, but this monster will never be satiated.

Mary Shelley warned us about such monsters in her chilling novel *Frankenstein*. What did this ambitious and overly-confident doctor create? A monster, of course, and it hunted him to the very ends of the earth after destroying all he held near and dear. Is it possible that we are witnessing the turning of the monster at places like Evergreen State? I'm not so sure this is an apt comparison, for Frankenstein's monster was eloquent, dedicated, and focused. The Social Justice Beast spawned on our liberal campus is not nearly as sophisticated.

The liberals may have inadvertently, however, awakened another monster. Shall we ask these Doctors Frankenstein on our various campuses if they are prepared to meet this yawning, stretching beast; for once his wrath is awakened it may well hunt them to the frozen ends of the earth. They have created a reactionary monster, you see, awakened the proverbial blonde beast, and perhaps created a fervent racism where there was none. When they try to shut down the beast by screaming *racist* how should it respond? Shelley's monster knows. He might say,

> "Come, my enemy; we have yet to wrestle for our lives; but many hard and miserable hours must you endure until that period shall arrive."*

Revenge is a dish best served cold and once this beast is awakened the Wrath of the Awakened Saxon will yawn and stretch at its side. It will happen slowly,

"...for they were not easily moved; they were icy willing to wait, til every count should be proved, 'ere the Saxon began to hate."**

Such a monster may never have hated again if not told that such was the essence of his being. On campuses nationwide, we hear the screeching *whiteness is oppression*. The blonde beast of yesteryear had gone peacefully to sleep but the screams for social justice have disturbed its slumber. There is no safe space from such an awakened beast. When students and professors yell *racist! bigot! phobic!* they may well awaken something best left sleeping. Let sleeping dogs lie? Yes, we should, but it may be too late.

http://legalinsurrection.com/2017/06/evergreen-prof-bret-weinsteins-greatest-alleged-sin-not-suffering-in-silence/
*Shelley, Mary. *Frankenstein*. Countless versions available.
** Kipling, Rudyard. *The Wrath of the Awakened Saxon*.
http://www.europeanamericansunited.org/school1/Fiction/kipling/awakened.htm

Lament for a Lost Liberal:

See No Reason, Hear No Reason, Speak No Reason

It started more than thirty years ago. He was accepted into an Ivy League school and his little sister put him on a plane and said goodbye. Years later, she realized that the goodbye was permanent. He came home for visits, of course, but he wasn't the same. She wasn't the same. He was enlightened, progressive, better than she who had stayed behind. She was still Southern; he had left, gone far North to a big city. He was better than Little Sister.

Or so he reasoned. *Only he who leaves this place can be successful; the farther the better*, and this he still claims. Is he right? One can not argue if one is still in the South, if one does not have quite as many letters after one's name. Such a stubborn rebel is pariah in his world, and yet he tried for years to change the Little Sister he had left behind, tried to indoctrinate her, but she grew up and saw the cloud over him. She stayed away.

They tried to remain close, but he was already lost. She remembers each moment of sad realization, even the simple things. He was visiting for the holidays, a rock video was on in the background. It was WASP. *Do you know what that means*? He hissed. No, she answered. *It's White Anglo-Saxon Protestant and they are racist and hateful*, he spewed as if he had just spit out poison. She remembers wondering why it was bad to be white, Anglo-Saxon, or Protestant; for that is exactly what he was. Had he forgotten? This was the same blonde boy who read his Bible every morning. The same white boy who told her not to forget to say her prayers every night. This was the same green-eyed soul who descended directly from the Angles and the Saxons. Why was he ashamed of himself?

Years passed and it was more of the same. One Christmas, Little Sister recommended a book. He responded vehemently, *I'll never read that fascist trash*. A year later, he was reading that very book. Why? A colleague recommended it, and so he recommended it to Little Sister, having completely forgotten that she had read it long before it was fashionable. She knew then she could never compete with one deemed a "colleague."

More years passed and Big Brother seemed settled with the latest non-white boyfriend. No one in the family objected. No one was bothered. No one cared about his homosexuality. Still, we were backward Southerners. Still, his very young Asian boyfriend wanted to see all things Southern when he visited Atlanta the first time. Scarlet O'Hara? Let's go the museum! Still, Southerners were somehow racist in their minds even as they expressed shock and fear at all the black people around us. *There are so many black people. I'm standing behind you*, he said.

Little sister visited him in San Francisco and she noticed the difference in classes right away. All the brown people were driving buses, picking up trash, cleaning here and there. She asked, *Where do they live? You can barely afford this place.* Big Brother nonchalantly waved in the direction of the Oakland Bridge and answered, *Oh, all those people live over there.* Those people? In his mind it was reasonable to say that and at the same time excoriate the South for having racial tensions.

Just the same, Big Brother likes to travel and see where *those people* come from. Annually, he goes on planned tours with guides to expensive resorts all over the map. He calls this experience. He says he travels and knows what it is like out there. He says Little Sister should do the same, for if one rarely leaves the South one can not possibly have a learned opinion. Big Brother declares proudly that he knows what he is talking about; he does not live in a bubble like she does. Big Brother makes these assertions from his plush office on a liberal campus from a liberal city and it is the only job he has had since adulthood. In fact, he has been entrenched on a liberal campus since he first got on that plane. Big Brother just might be in a bubble after all.

Years pass. More of the same. Little sister expresses consternation at the overtly sexual spectacle gay pride parades have become. Big Brother says he can no longer take any more of her racism and bigotry. Big Brother says she is a Nazi. Big Brother refuses to try to reach her any more for her life is *a tragic loss*. She is still in the South and she *likes* it. She is a lost cause. Big Brother does not know that he has been lost for decades.

Non Serviam:

A Call for Rebels

Those who bear the blame for society's ills often form the backbone of that very society. Where would the lawyer be without the criminal? The businessman without the greedy public? The pious inquisitor without the witch? They'd degenerate into madmen and criminals in their own right, never mind that they often already are. Society has deemed their behavior acceptable while that of the reject is abomination. And thus we have established a code of conduct, defined by the very souls who'd dare break it.

Who are those rebels today? They could be anyone. They could be heroes. They could be the outspoken ones who don't give a god damn if their peers call them racist or xenophobic. They could be those who won't be silenced in the name of political correctness, for what good does such a silence do? None; it harms. Take the case of the critic of Islam, perhaps a former Muslim herself. When we silence this rebel in our irrational and selfish fear of being called phobic, racist, or intolerant, we may as well hold down the little girl who gets her child's vagina hacked off and stitched shut on the blessed altar of the almighty hymen. When we silence those who speak out against genuine misogyny, abuse, or religious terror, we silence those who have been killed or abused in its name. This is not liberalism. This is not enlightened tolerance. This is cowardice. This is collusion with barbarism and a slap in the face of those who have suffered in yet another prophet's infallible name.

Those putting their hands over our mouths don't want citizens speaking out against a religion or a race. They don't want freedom of speech! When theirs is taken away by the same brash minorities they foolishly defend, I don't want to hear a single grumbling complaint. Oh, but they will moan and groan. They'll ask *how did this happen* and they'll never see the part they played. When the feminist and the gay rights activist jump on the band wagon du-jour of today's so-called liberals and tell us we can't judge another culture end up raped, stoned, or beheaded by that very culture - a culture that openly condemns and abuses them - should we say I told you so? Some of us will. Some of us will defend them. And we start now by refusing to silence our dissent, by not caring one damn bit about political correctness, by saying NO.

Legend has it that Lucifer said no; *Non Serviam*, in fact. "I will not serve," is what he declared. Religious considerations aside, I'll spare you a lengthy diatribe on the evolution of this literary character and his parallels in other cultures. It must suffice to say that he is the penultimate rebel with a cause. In one version of this oft-told tale, he would not serve that which he deemed immoral. Nor will I. I will not bow down to those who advise me to cover myself lest I entice a rapist. I will not tolerate the genital mutilation of children or the practice of arranged marriages to little girls. I will not silence my voice to avoid offending those who scream *racist!* with every breath. Tolerance is one thing - and a beautiful thing - but bending over for each and every cultural group that admittedly and repeatedly violates basic human rights is another matter altogether. This I will not do. *Non Serviam*, I'll say, with every breath in me.

When society has gone awry, we need rebels to set it aright. *Non Serviam*. Say it. Repeat it. Live it.

Ancestral Inspiration

Shhhh, Listen! There are countless sources of inspiration in this world and I count ancestry as one such source. There isn't one individual figure I look up to, but rather the general march of my genetic past from one side of the Atlantic to the other and all the travails in between. The roots of my family tree may be in Northern Europe, but the branches extend clear into the deep South of that new country, the United States, where the settlers were brazen enough to throw off the king's chains and start an experiment in freedom that has sadly gone awry. What is happening to the country they built? It pains me to think that they might be watching. And yet, this is also a thought that inspires me to action.

Look around you as one event after another becomes a debacle of free speech inhibited. Look as our protests become riots. Look at our freedoms slipping away, one day at a time, a gradual drip of poison like an IV in every American soul. What would our great-grandparents say? Would they be horrified? The answer is a resounding YES. Something must be done to change that answer to a satisfied NO, and it must be done before it's too late.

After a recent encounter with a black "activist" on the streets of Atlanta, I sat down and thought about the young man involved. He was the typical sort that hovers downtown with nothing better to do - drooping but designer pants, loose Nikes, sideways ball-cap, cumbersome gold chains; we've all seen him, the contemporary urban black answer to Everyman and he was there by the dozens. The encounter was uneventful and I walked on, ignoring *stupid white girl* and *fucking honky*; just par for the downtown course. What would I have said to him given the chance? I would have asked him about his ancestors. I would have asked him what they thought about recent BLM protests (read *riots*).

I might have said, "Wake up! The proud African residing inside you is ashamed. Did your ancestors build their own village, create their unique culture, and try like hell to preserve it even through slavery so you could bitch and moan about white-washed Oscars? Will you continue to ignore the inner voice of the noble African chieftain who is your precious ancestor when you or a fellow protestor shatters a car window and takes a laptop? What did he say? Shhh… Listen! What did your great-grandfather say? Listen to him, the man who suffered under the Arkansas sun dreaming his descendants would be free. Does the cash handed to you at the pawn shop make it easier to ignore his voice? Is he proud of you?"

He might have responded, "You ain't nothing but a damn racist and I ain't listening to this bullshit." He might be right, but we all saw it happen; it made national news. Still, no one wants to SAY it.

Say this instead, "You don't have to listen to me; stop screaming racism and listen to your ancestors. Imagine them watching you today. They've put down their tools and looked up from the cotton fields and they see you in a hundred and fifty odd years, free. Are they proud of you? If you're not absolutely certain that the answer is a loud YES, you're doing something wrong."

Obviously, I don't imagine enslaved Africans when I think of my ancestors. I envision whites with bent, red necks from Germany, France, England, and Ireland, some "spirited" away as involuntary indentured servants (the nice way of saying slaves), others free but starving, others free and taking this new world for all it was worth. Most dug out a life in Appalachia, but just barely. Momma just barely surviving another childbirth, kids just barely scraping together enough to eat, Daddy just barely keeping the greedy banks away from the struggling farm. It was always just barely. My grandmother just barely survived scarlet fever while my grandfather just barely survived the war. Yes, always just barely. But they made it and here I am.

I must ask myself the same question I wanted to ask the young protestor - are my ancestors proud of me? I don't know. I thought about Uncle John Bell Hood, a feisty general who saw an arm and a leg sawed off on Southern battlefields only to tie himself to his horse and ride into the fray once again. Family rumor has it he retired to New Orleans after the misunderstood War of Northern Aggression and he lived there many years with his quadroon mistress. For him, the war wasn't about racism - the term hadn't even been invented yet. I know that, and I think he'd be proud of my knowledge; I know that damn war wasn't about slavery.

No, the War Between the States wasn't about black or white. It was about green, the green in those Southern fields and the green tucked away in those Southern wallets. That was the green coveted by the bankers pulling Lincoln's strings. They didn't care about the slaves; wage slavery is a more profitable venture, after all. It is here that I'd like to tell that young protestor that we have the same enemy. Your ancestors will tell you about our country's battles with the bankers. Let them inspire you to follow the money. Follow the bullets! Look up at the string pullers to find your true enemy, not at each other. Shhh, listen! They will tell you, We Have the Same Enemy.

Be inspired. Cut your strings.

Equality: The False God

Equality. This contentious notion will someday be remembered as the Greatest Lie Ever Told, but for now the masses remain under its spell. Heroes, however, have an inborn immunity and they will not be entangled for long. The Left can tear down every statue, censor every speech, even ban the best of our books, and yet true nobility of spirit will remain and it will grow restless. The noble among us will rebel and rip from their hearts and souls sticky strands of generational propaganda.

These elite souls will expose the so-called morals and legalities of modern society as the ill-intended creations of degenerates and thieves. When laws and moral standards are drafted by such scheming men they affect tyranny and the only solution is the sword of the hero who cuts through the tangled web with no thought to unravel the ungodly mess. This task is left for the historian of the future who sits between museum walls, the final destination for any society that bends a knee to the false god equality.

Is this the fate of the Western world? It will be, unless We the People admit the mistake we made when we pretended we were all the same. We should never have allowed the tired, the poor, the huddled masses, and the weak-willed to enter our shores. Here the mongrelized hordes were not elevated. Here, instead, the noble were darkly tarnished to match their forced fellows. Here folly was enshrined as progress. Progress, like equality, is a false god. It is surely past time we pulled them both from our shrines.

It is likewise past time to free our minds from the tangle of lies spun by those who would be our global masters, for those who scurry when the lights come on will deceitfully appeal to your kinder nature and do no more than state the obvious ~ no one should be bought and sold at any slavers' auction. We readily agree and yet what is not said is where the trap lies, for while we no longer haggle over sullen cargo at the slave markets of old, we admire our illusory progress even as we are ALL bought and sold by suited slavers on Wall Street.

The spinners who profited from the slave trade in bygone days are the same Wanderers who scurry from kingdom to kingdom today, selling lies of equality while silently pulling the strings of those who haven't the fortitude to cut them. The Wanderers are still spinning their webs, ensnaring the good-hearted who have forgotten their own strength because they have forgotten their own glorious past. They have forgotten that man was never equal and they are loathe to admit that if equality could be achieved, it would be with us already and would not need to be enforced at the point of a gun.

Equality in Nature, however, does not exist. Only force and tyranny can bring about any sort of equality and this at the expense of the strongest and brightest stars. If the one is dimmed, will the others shine more brightly? No. All will be doomed to fade with a fleeting twinkle, nothing more. There are far too many lackluster stars today, for we have foolishly encouraged them and they have predictably bred and bred again. The result is naught but an impoverished population of livestock begging for a shepherd who will keep Nature at bay. Nature, however, will not be denied and with so much prey it is certain that we are headed for an era of slaughter. Nature, however, has yet to decide the victorious predator. Which side of the fence are you on?

Charity Is Not a Virtue

There is something sinister in the bottom of that bowl of sticky rice handed so magnanimously to the hungry African. What is mixed in with that cheap, plentiful grain if not contempt, condescension, self-aggrandizement? Or is it a belittling pity disguised as charity? What would the downtrodden do without its hand-outs? Continue on as they always have, or starve. Such is the way of Nature, but that is not good enough for the charitable. What power lies in that simple bowl of rice that costs the bleeding heart next to nothing while the hungry and ignorant trades his soul for a few bites, just enough to stay alive after native skill is forgotten, just enough to keep the charade going year after year.

What have our generous, long-distance philanthropists done? Perpetuated the misery of what amounts to little more than a brown-skinned idea long enough to engender another generation of misery. What will the generous do with his playthings' offspring? Torture them just the same. I ask you, oh magnanimous urbanites with your *only a few cents a day* mail-order orphans, who are you really helping? You have done nothing more than keep the hungry alive long enough to birth another generation of slaves forced into modernity. What are they doing when the cameras are not around? Digging out diamonds for your temporary, childless wives? Mining the depths for your next generation of I-phones? Hacking and slashing at rubber trees for the tires under your luxury cars? Is that why you continue feeding them? It makes you feel good about yourself, those requisite post-cards of brown faces gleefully accepting hand-outs provided by your pennies a day, pennies that keep those brown hands working.

How wonderful of the privileged to modernize the third-world! The generous protest, but we are sending them to school! Why? So they, too, can become cogs in the first-world economy? Or so they can become wholly dissatisfied with their traditional way of life? Which handful of misery is the philanthropist holding out to them? Even the terminology betrays us – third world? Who are we to say they are third and who the hell decided we were first? Are we in a race to destroy the planet? If so, we are first indeed and what have the generous done? Spread the poison, one bowl of rice at a time, one indoctrinating schoolhouse at a time, one modern convenience at a time – all as a tribe's traditional way of life is washed away in a stream of oh-so-modern pollution.

The activist screams about racism, but acts as if the brown-skinned couldn't exist without his pity. The progressive asserts the equality of all, but tosses pennies to the African, the Guatemalan, the Afghan. The liberal asserts the beauty of diversity, but wants the brown shades bred up the color spectrum while the white shades are bred down. The modernist praises the multi-cult, but wants the Sudanese and the Indian to live just like him.

I say to these long-distance philanthropists: Walk away. Wash your hands of it. Your charity helps no one but global pillagers who offer a bowl of rice in exchange for a proud people's freedom while the tried and true ways of their ancestors are thrown into the garbage heap of modernity. If you truly care, if you truly believe in the multi-cult, diversity, and the beauty of the rainbow, leave them alone. If they are your equals, let them feed themselves. Let Nature work her will. She is wiser than you.

Inquisition at Nuremberg

For roughly 300-400 years the name of Jesus was not uttered by respectable citizens without a spit to the ground in revulsion. Likewise, for another 300-400 years, the word witch was not uttered without fear and disgust. Now the Christ is worshiped by millions and our children dress as witches for Halloween. To the point: words and titles shift in power or lose their power over the years. This is happening now with the oft-used misnomer NAZI. He's a Nazi, I'm a Nazi, wouldn't you like to be a Nazi too? One can all but hear the catchy jingle.

Thanks to hashtagging liberals and modern technology, the word Nazi will be redeemed, empowered, or rendered harmless very soon. This is partially due to over-usage and unfounded accusations hurled carelessly from small minds and big mouths. The Nazi transformation is also due, in larger part, to mountains of new information on the Third Reich and conversely damning information about the Allies. No longer does the historian worth a damn see good guys on one side and bad guys on the other as in a cheap board game. For decades, however, the story of the Second World War was one of good vs. evil, plain and simple. We know better now.

Take the Nuremberg trials for example. The time is fast approaching – and in some circles it has already arrived – when we will see this so-called trial for the farce it was. We will come to call it a modern-day Inquisition, complete with extreme tortures, false allegations, false confessions, tainted evidence, skewed and biased judges, and a pre-determined damned if you do/damned if you don't outcome. This all sounds like something out of the dungeons of the seventeenth century, and yet this was less than one hundred years ago and reads more like a work of prescient science fiction.

In Nuremberg, we have thought crimes manifest in piles of ash that have not been ceremoniously swept to the four winds as in the town squares of late medieval Europe but oddly preserved by those whose livelihood depends on the narrative as it is presented in victor-penned textbooks. In these pages, the truth was erased and rewritten to match the prepared tales of survivors and so-called experts. The ash was mixed into the victors' ink and the flesh became the word, Holy Writ that is not to be challenged. When contrary evidence began to surface, as it inevitably does, we saw Orwellian scenes of denial in which the revisionist might say, *I saw that! You changed the picture!* The answer is *What picture. There is no picture.** And round and round we go even as the revisionist is beaten and jailed, like a German witch.

The witch hunts were absolute horrors and the trials a travesty of justice; but we know that now. And Nuremberg? A show trial, nothing more. We know the Nazi defendants were tortured, even permanently maimed, to extract confessions; we also know that confessions obtained under torture are not reliable. We know documents were forged. We know defense attorneys were not allowed to admit mountains of evidence. We know a certain narrative had to be fed to a hungry public and so it was. Perhaps the most glaring truths are the war crimes committed by the allies, swept under a proverbial rug by every 1950's housewife. With time, all those rotting German corpses have begun to stink and can be hidden no longer. As many historians have said, the truth will out. **

These historians, of course, are rejected, even fined, beaten, harassed, and arrested; but why? So many questions and they had the nerve to ask them, that's why. Asking questions is not denial. True denial is denying one's right to ask questions, denying information, denying freedom of speech. These are the deniers and true to form they will point fingers and accuse you of doing that which colors their guilt. Should you even raise your hand you are shot down as an anti-semite. That is denial. Historical inquiry is not denial. What we need to ask ourselves regarding the Holocaust is not why did it happen but rather why are we not allowed to investigate it even today. Perhaps too much is riding on the narrative as it is presented in our schools and mass media. If it crumbled, would Israel's right to exist likewise crumble? When it is bad for one's agenda if less people died, one's agenda may be rightly called suspicious.

*Orwell, George. *1984*. Countless editions available. Read one!
**Adapted from: Summers, Rachel. *The Forgetting*. Create Space: 2017.
https://www.amazon.com/Forgetting-Mission-Maligned-4/dp/1976412994/ref=asap_bc?ie=UTF8
For more, please listen to the following from Guerrilla Radio:
https://www.youtube.com/watch?v=-O7-zQeuk4U

What Color Is Your Friday?

It happens every year, Black Friday, the day retailers go "into the black" in their accounts. For this to happen, countless consumers go into the red in their already cinched-tight household budgets. Debt, debt, debt and the consumer is willingly bled dry with each swipe of the card. Blu-Rays, laptops, I-phones – the list is endless and the cost high but what is it all for? Nothing. This is meaningless. One might argue that X wants a new video game; it will make X happy! Perhaps little X should have been taught to value something of value.

This is madness. I hereby declare today any color but black. Why not a beautiful Green Friday, a day spent enjoying the wonders of the green world? Go for a walk, discover something, enjoy the November air and you will see it – flaming beauty everywhere. Orange, yellow, red, and all the colors of Autumn. Take in the swirling browns and grays on the trunk of a gnarled oak who has seen empty stores come and go.

If shop you must, then do so with a rebel's heart. Go to that dark and dank used bookshop you have passed so many times – there are precious worlds tucked away between those cracked leather covers. Go to that crooked farmer's stand on that empty corner and discover jams and jellies canned the way your grandmothers would have canned and spread some tradition this year. Go to an out-of-the-way historic site and visit the gift shop – you may learn something about your own past that you can pass along and brighten the holidays for years to come. There are countless ways around garish commercialism.

Nonetheless, madness will ensue today and hereafter. Somewhere, a few seconds ago, a shopper took a right elbow to the gut over a gaming console and there is only one reason why – both of these credulous consumers are empty inside. Only those unsatisfied in their very souls are so desperate. They look without to avoid the void within. If you have meaning, true meaning, in your life you do not need fad clothes, gadgets and gizmos, or gaming escapism. Conspicuous consumption is for those who have nothing better to show the world. Show us your true colors! Is it only black?

I assert that there is a world of color in all of us, but one must dig to find these gems and sometimes the digging hurts. Dig anyway. Black Friday is all about greed. Grab, grab, grab and all of it is useless. This or that somnambulist shopper amassing video games, movies, new phones, I-pods, designer clothes, laptops, whatever is on sale! Money, money, money and all of it wasted on nothing that matters. Is this the American Dream? No, this is more of a nightmare.

Nightmares, dear reader, wake one with a jolt. Perhaps that is what we need. Some will surely continue to dream, continue to want, continue to grab at anything under a blinking neon sign. Others, however, are wide awake, painfully aware, and not interested in the latest this or that nonsense. These are the barbarians already inside the gates and they will not go quietly into that black night. No, they will make a noise never to be forgotten. Perhaps a rebel yell, something to awaken the greedy consumer from his frenzied slumber and let the light shine in. There you will see it – color. There are so many colors this day can be. Keep the black in your account, let the stores sit empty, and enjoy your colorful world. It is right in front of you.

Hanukkah and the Case of the Hellenic Heils

Another year has passed and the last of the Hanukkah candles has been lit, but what do we know about this rival winter holiday? It was not until the 19th century that Hanukkah became popular, largely because Jewish children felt left out during the Christmas season, or so the story goes. What is this holiday about, exactly? The First and Second Books of Maccabees give us most of our information on this Jewish holiday revolving around the so-called "Revolt of the Maccabees."

The short version: the Seleucid king over Judea, Antiochus IV, suddenly and inexplicably developed a raging case of anti-Semitism for no reason. He then insisted that everyone follow the same Hellenic customs. To discourage foreign religions, he had pigs sacrificed in the Jewish temple, banned circumcision, and murdered Jews who clung to their religious traditions. Hence the revolt in which the victimized Jews defeated near diabolical forces.
And non-Jewish sources? Obscure at best, but not impossible. What happened before Antiochus IV gave the Hellenic Heil? The Jews instigated a local rebellion while he was invading Egypt. This alone would provoke antagonism, but there is more – namely corrupt Jews pulling political strings. The highest office was that of the High priest. Onias was High Priest at the time of the rebellion, but his brother Jason wanted the title and bribed Antiochus into giving it to him, but there is more – another schemer, Menelaus, offered an even larger bribe and so he was made High Priest.

Jason was none too pleased with this and when he heard the false rumor that Antiochus IV had been killed, he called together his forces and attacked rival Jews; this was the "revolt" that put the Seleucid king over the edge. This was not an oppressed peoples vying for religious freedom but simple infighting over power, politics, and money. Thus the foundation was laid and soon, others jumped into the fray. Enter the Maccabees, an essentially fundamentalist group who rejected all things Greek, including their policy of settling non-Jews in Jewish lands. Diversity? Multiculturalism? Not here, said Antiochus' Jewish subjects.

Of course, we hear the same rejection of immigration into Jewish lands even today. Modern Israelites, like the Maccabees, wanted their territory to remain Jewish. In this sense, Hanukkah could be viewed as a reminder to put the tribe above all else. The rebels of the Second Century BCE certainly did. Judas Maccabeus led several battles in which the Jews defeated the Greeks, largely because the Greek army was divided on two fronts and did not take the Jewish threat too seriously, not until the rebels captured Jerusalem and rededicated the Temple – this is when the eight day holiday was first celebrated.*

Two short-lived kings later and the Jewish rebels were finally defeated, but Hanukkah lived on. Two centuries later and the story of the eight miraculous days of oil found its way into the legends via the Talmud; it is this miracle of light-bringing oil that is reflected in the lighting of the Menorah. Today, Jerusalem is still a hotbed of contention with high-powered Jews vying for control over temples and taxes while the surrounding areas are lit ablaze in one war after another.

Hanukkah – is it a reminder of past Jewish political intrigue and double standards or a symbol of the unending perpetuation of the same?

*https://www.haaretz.com/jewish/features/1.630770

Kwanzaa: Made in America

This morning marks the fourth day of Kwanzaa, a holiday passed off as something authentically African and even ancient, but that is simply not the case. Kwanzaa began in 1966 in California. Its creator is one Maulana Ndabezitha Karenga (his real name is Ronald Everett), who is now a 75-year-old professor of African studies at California State University, Long Beach. In 1976 Karenga received a Ph.D. from United States International University (now a for-profit institution called Alliant International University). He received another Ph.D. from the University of Southern California in 1994.

With such accolades, Karenga seems qualified to create a holiday, but this illustrious fellow has received other honors as well – namely a conviction for felony sexual assault and a diagnosis of schizophrenia and paranoia. He was convicted in 1971 for torturing and assaulting two women who were members of his radical, paramilitary, black nationalist group called United Slaves, a rival to the Black Panthers. In fact, members of Karenga's tribe were convicted of murdering two Panthers. The murders occurred in 1969 when the Slaves and the Panthers were fighting over which group would control the then-new Afro-American Studies Center at UCLA. (What a great job California schools are doing. Just this week farmers' markets were declared racist by two UC San Diego professors. Whatever would we do without the wisdom of these sages?).

Back to Karenga's conviction. Deborah Jones said she and Gail Davis were whipped with an electrical cord and beaten with a karate baton. Both women were nude for the beatings. They were also burned with a soldering iron and had detergent and running hoses put in their mouths. Why? Magic rocks. Karenga believed that the women were using crystals to poison him. A psychiatrist declared Karenga to be both paranoid and schizophrenic.

What does this have to do with Kwanzaa? A quick internet search of "Kwanzaa History" never mentions any of the above. Instead, the reader will learn that the recently concocted holiday is a pan-African celebration of family, community and culture, observed from December 26 through January 1. The word itself is Swahili and means "first fruits." Kwanzaa, according to generic web, has its roots in the harvest celebrations of historic African cultures and civilizations. The seven principles of Kwanzaa are: unity, self-determination, collective work, cooperative economics, purpose, creativity and faith in ourselves.

Add the word "rape" to the search and you will find out so much more. Those seven seemingly innocent principles, for instance, are carbon copies of those of the ill-famed Symbionese

Liberation Army. Yes, the same group that robbed banks and murdered here and there as well as the kidnappers of the famous newspaper heiress Patty Hearst in 1974. So much for having principles.

Come any New Years Day, none of this will matter. Kwanzaa has slowly but surely become a joke even among African-Americans who prefer the very Euro-centric traditions of Christmas, which are closely tied, of course, to the pagan Yule and even Saturnalia – white holidays, all of them. Perhaps a sincere advocate for the so-called African diaspora should invent a genuinely African holiday rather than a spiteful spin-off. Better yet, African-Americans, some of the staunchest pro-Christians left in this country, should celebrate Christmas without apology. As should any other believer.

Education and Academia

Matter Over Mind

As early as 1861, one of America's great thinkers, Ralph Waldo Emerson, smelled something foul in Academia. In *The Celebration of the Intellect* he tells us that,

> "Harvard College has no voice in Harvard College, but State Street [the financial/political interests] votes it down on every ballot. Everything will be permitted there, which goes to adorn Boston Whiggism – is it geology, astronomy, poetry, antiquities, art, rhetoric? But that which exists for, to be a fountain of novelties out of heaven, a Delphos uttering warning and ravishing oracles to lift and lead mankind – that it shall not be permitted to do or think of. On the contrary, every generosity of thought is suspect and has a bad name. And all the youths come out decrepit citizens; not a prophet, not a poet, not a daimon, but is gagged and stifled or driven away."

And now, to make matters worse, our universities have safe spaces where a giant child can go and spend quality time coloring rainbows or rolling out Play Dough if another giant child hurts his or her or whatever's feelings. Now we have epic rants over pronouns. Now we have students screaming *cocks not glocks*. Now we have so-called POC students blocking white students from going to class even as these same POC students get scholarship money not for any sort of actual scholarship but for being a few shades darker than whitey who pays or doesn't go to school; this they pass off as white privilege. How is any of this passing for education?

The better question might be this: How is it that a small group of international financiers has been in control of our rotten university system for more than a century now and so few of us have protested? What business have they running our schools? Big business; that's the answer. Around the time of World War One, Evans Clark, a preceptor at Princeton University (who was fired for daring to voice his findings) discovered that "bankers, manufacturers, merchants, public utility officers, financiers, great publishers, and lawyers" made up more than half of the boards of every school he surveyed. There were no basic labor representatives at all. Not a single professor was a board member at the college where he or she taught and only a tiny percentage served at all.

The board, of course, determines the direction or "theme" of the university. When that board is made up of individuals whose priorities lie in their bank accounts, we have every right to question their motives and likely self-serving agendas. Evans Clark's conclusion, before he was relieved of his job, was that,

"We have allowed the education of our youth to fall into the absolute control of a group of men who represent not only a minority of the total population but have, at the same time, enormous economic and business stakes in what kind of an education it shall be."

Other dissenters around Clark's time thought socialism might be the answer to this capitalist take-over of our schools; news of the horrors of Bolshevism hadn't yet made it over the sea. Slowly but surely, our schools slipped into a Marxist grip and what is the result? International financiers are still sitting on the board and different labels are slapped atop the same agendas. We are indebted for years as students are coddled and rendered useless. The value of an education goes down as the price goes up. Challenging the status quo will earn you not a degree but walking papers. Don't rock the yacht! Capitalists, socialists; the elite at the top don't care what you call them. They are the puppet masters and we are being played.

Missing the Mark

Here is a brief summary of the students in a typical middle-school classroom: These few have to take pills just to function, or so they are told. These few are overweight and miserable at the ripe old age of twelve. These few can't put down their smart phones. These few are raging bundles of energy because they are expected to sit still and be quiet all day. These other few are bored out of their minds. The teacher is trying to teach, but no one is interested. Why? Maybe they learned this last year, or maybe last quarter, and no new challenge is brought forth. Maybe the curriculum is so disconnected from everything else they are learning that they don't see the significance. Maybe it's this way in their next period as well.

We are doing something wrong. My sons have never been challenged by any of their teachers. Not once. If they have read the classics, it is because I gave them books. If they know who Machiavelli and Dante are, it is because those names are familiar in our house. So what are they doing at school all day? Ridiculing their lackluster teachers on Instagram. Arguing with these same teachers over the nonsense that is common core mathematics. Being sent to the principal's office for gutting a textbook and gluing a copy of *The Hobbit* inside the cover just to have something to do. They are bored.

We are underestimating our children. They do not need medication to pay attention – they need something interesting to engage their minds. They need to be challenged. They need suitable outlets for both mental and physical energy. The model for Classical Education may provide what they need. Divided into three phases of four years each, the Classical Education model repeats instruction of various subjects rooted in the major historical cycles but within those phases the approach to those cycles is altered to meet the growing demands of the developing mind.

Take mythology, for instance. Children love these stories and should hear them from a variety of cultures at a young age. This is when the foundation is laid and the stories are memorized not by recitation but by hearing them in different contexts, by playing games, by building a small Trojan Horse, by enjoying and even imitating what they are learning. In the next phase, a more literate approach is welcomed and by the third phase, the original texts are easily absorbed and engaged. Look to Homer's *Odyssey*. If this is taught from day one, any graduate will know the story well. He will know how it influenced western civilization. He will know how it influences story-tellers even today. Add to this hands-on experience, like stringing a stiff bow as in the closing scene, or building a scale model of a Greek ship, and that story will resonate for life.

Why is that important? Our civilization is based on our Classics. If we undermine our foundation, we fall. If we understand our foundation and build on it accordingly, we thrive. Understanding the past is key to understanding the present and that is how a better future is made. This seems such common sense that it should not be an issue, and yet countless times my son has come home and told me he just watched a video in class. Image learning is passive. Image learning is not a challenge to most minds. Engaging a text on a page and bringing it to life oneself is a challenge, and that is how minds grow. Connecting this story to that story across subjects and eras is a challenge, and that is how minds are sharpened.

Sharpen your children's minds as you sharpen a blade. Sharpen your arrows! Go outside and shoot. Tell them about the Battle for Agincourt, a battle won by archers and immortalized in Shakespeare's *Henry V*. History, literature, theater, politics, and what might be a life-saving skill have just been learned. These are the moments young minds remember. If the schools are not providing these moments, make them yourself. Sharpen those blades before another dulls them to uselessness.

http://www.telegraph.co.uk/news/uknews/11946012/Henry-V-St-Crispins-Day-speech-in-full.html

Standardized Students:

School - An Assembly Line for the Masses

Modern education, from pre-school through grad school, is designed to destroy the imagination, to cull free thinkers, and to mass produce mindless graduates easily controlled and manipulated. Why? Independent adults who think and do for themselves would bring down the walls of this corrupted civilization. We would see at last that it was nothing but a house of cards. We would see at last the proverbial man behind the curtain. We would see at last our strings and the puppeteers who pulled them.
Our schools should be sacred space, where we

> "fill the young of the species with knowledge and awaken their intelligence…
> Nothing could be further from the truth. The aim…is simply to reduce as many
> individuals as possible to the same safe level, to breed and train a standardized citizenry,
> to put down dissent and originality. That is its aim in the United States
> and that is its aim everywhere else."*

Disheartening, isn't it? We spend our most energetic and curious years - the years we are the most receptive and alive - sitting in desks, indoors, being domesticated, tamed, and finally broken. If you do not comply? You are considered a failure. So, we'd better take those standardized tests seriously; think about that word, standardized. They are testing our children to ensure that they are becoming standardized.

None of us came out of the womb with a model number that matched hundreds if not thousands of the same batch. This is not *A Brave New World*. We are born individuals and we should do our damnedest to stay that way, all modern notions of success to the contrary. Success is not letters after your name or numbers in your account. Success is happiness, fulfillment, and purpose. Success is physical and mental health. Success is not only what we change, but what we allow to remain the same. To teach our children otherwise is to do them a grave disservice.

We are doing ourselves and our children a disservice when we passively allow our corrupted education system to shut down the reality of who we are and what we are capable of becoming. The vast majority of our programmed teachers are a product of this corrupted system and are defeated before they begin. Should one of them stray outside the box a reprimand is in order. Should this actual teacher dare to make it a habit, he or she will be unemployed. Good teachers are few and far between and most resign before they're fired. I know one such teacher; he told me it was hopeless.

I don't agree. In the words of another troublesome teacher, John Taylor Gatto, we can encourage our children to take an education rather than receive a schooling. We can meet the other parents, collectively refuse copious amounts of mind-numbing homework, tell our kids to turn off the damn televisions and video games and go outside and get dirty. We can encourage imagination, encourage questions, encourage wandering and wondering. Say no to all the electronic nonsense our children are conditioned to want; and say no to it ourselves. Don't go to a movie. Go on a hike. Read to them. Buy books and balls, not Playstations. In short, act like you give a damn.

*H.L. Mencken in *The American Mercury*, April 1924.

Erased:

Filling in the Missing Pieces

Mother: Have you learned about the Holocaust in school?

Son: Yeah, of course. We talked about it a lot. We read books and watched movies.

Mother: Did they talk about the Holodomor too?

Son: What's that?

A typical response. As I write this, the computer's spell checker has likewise never heard of the Holodomor, that rarely mentioned episode of Ukranian history in which up to ten million died of deliberately imposed starvation or were exiled to Russia's infamous gulags. Why the historical blank? In a grossly oversimplified nutshell, our educational system peddles but one socially accepted narrative and all else falls by the wayside. It is this way from noon naps to doctoral dissertations with much left out in between.

Year after year earning a history degree, a master's degree, even beyond, and I had never heard of the Holodmor either. I never knew there had been such a high percentage of white slaves in the American colonies. I never knew the Bolsheviks were largely Jewish. No, none of this was ever mentioned in the many, many classrooms I'd sat in day after day. And so, the question looms ever larger: Why the historical blank?

Perhaps more to the point is this question: Why have the academics betrayed us? These are the brave souls meant to sharpen humanity's most valuable weapon, our minds, and yet they haven't sharpened anything for decades now. They can't, for they are not allowed to be sharp, to challenge accepted views, or to be creative. Consider the divide between academic and non-academic writers.

> "Many [professors] are now troubled by 'a writer who works up his own notions and
> signs his own name.' For the literary man in college…the literary

man [outside] presents himself as the distant inhabitant of another intellectual world; and
he figures as the final installment of the body of material to be studied."*

The academic has no ideas of his own; he regurgitates the thoughts of others. We must abandon
this false smith when we discover the painful truth that today's academics were all conceived in
1984 and they've no intention of sharpening a damned thing. Oh no! It's their state sanctioned
task not only to piss on our blades and dull them to utter uselessness but to keep us from battle,
pretending there's no war being fought. There is, and the losses are staggering, for the territory is
your mind. The academic has been compromised.

Likewise, the educator has scarcely been educated. Here is a typical university scenario: Most
students only read assigned texts. They stay well within the confines of the class discussion.
Most won't give any of it a second thought until forced to dredge it up in an assignment, and
they'll be prompted in that essay. They'll turn a trite phrase or two just to make the required
word count. They'll curb any urge to creativity when churning out one formulaic assignment
after another because they'll be reprimanded for daring to write outside the box. Thoroughly
indoctrinated, perhaps designated a doctor, they'll then take their magic pieces of paper and work
day after identical day to maintain a false prestige, a meaningless existence, a "respectable"
lifestyle. If they're successful, they'll publish and not perish even as they forge another false
generation. If they don't toe the line, they may never receive tenure and piles of applicants are
eagerly waiting to take their coveted place.

In the above scenario, can true education take place? No. Most academics fall in line without
question; for most have had the questions programmed out of them. When that celebrated
professor gets home in the evenings, she'll probably grade a stack of papers, making sure the
young writers are being properly programmed as well. Click, click, click. Gears in a machine.
This is life for most of us. It's time to ask why. Tomorrow, and tomorrow, and tomorrow. Must
we continue to creep through this pettiness day after day? Must we continue this way to the last
syllable of recorded time? No, and no, and no.

There are historical blanks in our education because we are educated to fit a certain mold. If we
knew those who play the victim card also had stacks of villain cards tucked up their tailored
sleeves, we may no longer listen to their lamentations. If we knew those most often accused of
villainy had as many scars on their backs as our media-favored downtrodden, we may no longer
feel such guilt. If we knew, we may no longer fall in line.

And so there are blanks, so many blanks. What is the Holodomor? Ten million souls, erased.

*Jacoby, Russel. *The Last of the Intellectuals: American Culture in the Age of Academe*. Basic Books, NY, NY:
1987.

From Dungeon to Tower:

The Kingdom Is Rotten

Walk with me from depths of the blackened Dungeon to the heights of the Ivory Tower and, if you are among those with eyes to see and ears to hear, you will see that even these extremes are ruled over by the self-same ilk. These are the thinkers trained to indoctrinate us from pre-school to grad school with warm and tender thoughts of multiculturalism, diversity, and universal acceptance. At the same time we are instilled with an absolute horror of racism, bigotry, and intolerance - as they define such abstractions, of course.

What, you may ask, is wrong with a kingdom that pushes the above values? *Acceptance good…intolerance bad*, we grunt like Hollywood cavemen taught a few words that we sound off by rote like mind-numbing mantras, with no understanding of what we are mouthing. Just say the words. Just agree with the nice man in the suit at the front of the classroom. When he points his finger accusingly, when he screams *Nazi, Racist, Bigot*, just go along with it. He is respected; he has suede elbow patches and extra letters after his name! If he says Mr. X is bad because Mr. X does NOT feel shame when he sees his white skin, then surely Mr. X is, in fact, a very bad man.

In this kingdom, there is no room for those of pale visage. This is not a university. No, this is a multiversity and the white has been washed from the Ivory Tower. Still, the question remains. What is wrong with tolerance, acceptance, and diversity? Nothing, per se. The problems lie in the motives. Our students are taught these values not to promote harmony but to promote cultural rot; the culture in question is, of course, white European culture.

White students are taught that their traditions are inherently hateful and best left between museum walls or, better yet, forgotten entirely. Religion, mythology, literature, even music grown from European soil is harshly cut down in the worst case this world has yet seen of "tall poppy syndrome." Do you like Wagner? You must be a Fascist. Do you enjoy Norse mythology? You must be a Nazi. Yes, I have personally experienced these accusations for an offense no greater than reading Icelandic sagas and listening to German opera. Such accusations are hurled from small minds and big mouths - and the loudest of these can be found in our rotten schools.

Institutions of cultural transmission, like our schools, have an enormous responsibility to preserve the culture that created them, not to cause its slow rot. And yet here we are at a point in history where students at the best universities in this tottering kingdom don't want to read the classics of English literature because they were written by white men. This is poison and it is being deliberately administered in the name of multiculturalism, diversity, and tolerance.

We are indeed at a most absurd juncture when national history becomes a taboo.

> "Every reference to ancestral culture, suspected of damaging the dignity and respect of non-natives, must be banished from the political, pedagogical, and cultural discourse. Art

implodes. One can even imagine that the statuary that adorns the facade of institutions, modeled on the nation's ethnic type, may disappear into the depths of museums."*

Yes, this is happening.

I recently spoke with a student at one of our prestigious universities and she was frustrated to say the least. This is what she told me: "Something needs to be done about all this racial nonsense. I wanted to do a paper in Modern Western Civ about my recent German ancestry but no! I was told it was too sensitive a subject. My great- grandparents lived through that damn war and I mean just barely. They weren't Nazis. They weren't even soldiers. Just people trying to survive one bomb after another and I can't talk about that because someone might get offended? There was another student in that same class who wrote something about his grandfather's involvement in the Civil Rights movement. He was a Black Panther, but somehow that's ok. Really? What happened to our professors that they can't see the blatant double standard here? It's fucking ridiculous."

Yes it is, Student X. Yes it is. In this rotten kingdom, however, where the walls are so rotten they've turned inside-out, it surely makes perfect sense. Diversity, acceptance, and tolerance for all - except you.

*Krebs, Pierre. *Fighting for the Essence*. Arktos Media, 2012, p. 71.

Wanderers In Our Midst:

The Forgetting and the Deliberate Erosion of Tradition

There are trespassers in the Ivory Tower; Wanderers who have taken up residence where they do not belong. These maleficent Wanderers have cast a spell of somnambulistic *Forgetting* on the kingdom whose inhabitants forget day by day and bit by bit who they are and where they came from, thus becoming ever more malleable as serfs unaware that they exist in service to these wailing Wanderers.

This is no fairy tale; this is really happening even as our fairy tales are slowly forgotten. Likewise pushed into forgetfulness is myth, fable, tradition; anything that reminds the serfs that they are more than what the wanderers want them to be. This forgetfulness begins early for the serfs when they are sent to schools controlled by the wanderers who label tradition and culture as backward, irrelevant, even racist.

That word and its equivalents - racist, racism, bigot, phobic - is one of their most powerful spells; shutting down any protests the serfs may have otherwise proposed, shutting down even friendly conversation. As a serf looks to his own past as a matter of pride, a Wanderer or another serf will scream *racist*, and the seeker searches no more. Piece by piece and tale by tale, the serfs' past is lost. His roots are severed. He is homeless and thus easily controlled by the Wanderers who hold fast their tales and traditions wherever they may roam. In fact, these Wanderers gradually supplant the serfs' culture with their own, teaching their tall tales to the masses who are trained not to question the accepted narrative lest they be branded as hateful, phobic or anti~. In some parts of this vast kingdom, those who'd dare ask questions are thrown into dungeons for their daring, all at the will of the Wanderers whose message must be accepted or else.

The Wanderers residing in the Tower teach a carefully selected handful of serfs to promulgate their message to those students who can pay the price and learn their Newspeak. Those who continue to use the vernacular and speak to the average serf are not selected for this task, rather they are burned at the stake of scholarly opinion whilst their would-be colleagues whisper amongst themselves as if a fun-house mirror image of medieval ecclesiasts holding tight their Vulgates even as Tyndal* writhes in flames and the varied tales of the serfs' are labeled superstitious, out-dated, dead on the desk.

Forget the past! It's all about progress, and progress is the Wanderers' word of choice, pushed daily in one classroom after another until the next generations' students - you, me, finally our children - know nothing of the old gods, the witch in the wood, or the hero on a white horse. No, these are forgotten, pushed aside for something new, as is the entire literary and philosophical tradition of the West. The serfs' classics are deemed racist, irrelevant, and best forgotten.

In just a few generations, the serfs' most cherished tales pass into oblivion.

> "The effective loss of cultural traditions on such scale makes talk of a new Dark Ages far
> from frivolous," **

and book burnings an event we should come to expect. When the highest echelons of education cry that they do not want to read English literature in an English literature class - and only because the once celebrated authors are all white males - tradition is rendered null and void. When philosophy students cry that Plato and Aristotle are old-fashioned and irrelevant, even too European, culture is rendered null and void. When standards are lowered to accommodate the crying serfs of another class, the value of an education is rendered null and void.

This is precisely the goal of the Wanderers who, of course, never call us serfs for they don't want us to know what we have slowly become. They don't want us to hear the old meanings of our words when they twist the definitions. They don't want us to see the erosion of our own values. They don't want us to speak about our own past and its rich heritage. Hear no evil, see no evil, speak no evil? Yes, but most significantly, they do not want us to know that there is indeed a man behind the proverbial curtain, pulling our strings. He is there; we can see him clearly for he has become far too confident. We know that he and the majority of his comrades are Wanderers and we know what they are doing. The question is, what will we do about it? The Wanderer will not know the answer until it hits him in the face.

* The Vulgate is the Latin translation of the bible used in the Catholic Church throughout most of the Middle Ages. Tyndal was an English scholar burned at the stake for translating the Bible into English so that the common folk could read it themselves.

** Lasch, Christopher. The Culture of Narcissism: American Life in an Age of Diminishing Expectations. Norton and CO., 1991, p.150-151.

Cultural Marxism:

The Undermining of a Civilization's Soul

The corruption starts at an early age and is fully admitted by those who know they are involved. In 1951, for instance, Bertrand Russell confessed in *The Impact of Science on Society*,* that the teachers of the future will "try different methods of producing an unshakable conviction that snow is black." They will discover that "home is obstructive", that indoctrination must begin "before the age of ten", and the "opinion that snow is white must be held to show a morbid taste for eccentricity." He goes on to assert that "every government that has been in charge of education for a generation will be able to control its subjects securely without the need of armies or policemen."

While the latter assertion has yet to manifest, far too many of our fellow citizens are screaming that snow is black and condemning in one way or another those who see white. If one doesn't see black by the time of college enrollment, chances are one soon will. For the past sixty years, the manicured lawns of our colleges and universities have witnessed words manipulated, ideas promulgated, and thoughts implanted with the sole aim of undermining one piece of Western Civilization at a time. In fact, since the 1960's a "hostile, adversary elite has emerged to dominate intellectual and political debate. It is an elite that almost instinctively loathes the traditional institutions of European-American culture."**   Agreed, though I'd leave out the word "almost".

Does this sound far too conspiratorial, paranoid even? Rewind to 1922, Russia, when Lenin called a meeting to discuss the advancement of Marxism as a cultural movement. Present at this meeting was a certain Willi Munzenberg who actually proposed "to organize the intellectuals and use them to make Western Civilization stink. Only then, after they have corrupted all its values and made life impossible, can we impose the dictatorship of the proletariat." By 1924 Stalin was in power and he kicked these conspiring intellectuals to the curb, which turned out to be Frankfurt University. Here began the Frankfurt School, which Hitler closed down when he came to power. Those involved didn't quit. No, they dispersed to various universities in the United States. Now they call it the Institute for Social Research.

Munzenberg did a fine job summing up their long-term goals when he said, "We will make the West so corrupt that it stinks."

In Sean McMeekin's *The Red Millionaire: A Political Biography of Willi Munzenberg*, we read that this wayward intellectual was "the perpetrator of some of the most colossal lies of the modern age."*** These lies include the gender-less, race-less, faith-less, class-less nonsense we now hear everywhere we turn. -Less is more to the corrupted intellectual who sees the masses as a name-less, face-less commodity and nothing more.

Do you want -less or do you want more? I want more and I will fight for it.

*Russell, Bertrand. *The Impact of Science on Society.* Routledge (reprint): 2016.
**MacDonald, Kevin. *The Culture of Critique: An Evolutionary Analysis of Jewish Involvement...* First Books Library, 2002.
***McMeekin, Sean. *The Red Millionaire: A Political Biography of Willi Munzenberg.* Yale University Press, 2004.

Blood and Memory

The Ivory Tower is crumbling, and it pains me to admit it. It was a slow realization, one that began in a Classics course. At that same time I was in an archery class and the day we had to string a longbow was the day we read the bow stringing scene at the end of the *Odyssey*, when Odysseus comes home and challenges his wife's suitors to string his famous bow. I'd read it before, but I'd never understood the significance of that scene until I had to actually get my hands on a bow and do it. When I saw my bloody fingers I realized something - this is how you teach. You get up and walk away from the desk and bring those dead letters to life! I practiced this myself over the next few years and then submitted a proposal to my dean to get the untried students out of their desks and into the world; I was co-teaching a class on Olympic Religions and I wanted to actually do some of the sports involved. I was denied immediately and with a dismissive laugh. Insurance was the reason. Incidentally, I did my presentation on the marathon and ran a marathon myself to the utter disbelief of students and professor alike.

Have we become such weaklings, such sniveling cowards? Did the Olympic gods ask for insurance, or did they want blood? I gave them blood in that race and I will never forget the significance. Nothing, absolutely nothing, heard or read will outweigh something experienced. Nothing.

The Ivory Tower no longer provides experience. It houses dead letters on flat paper. Anyone with enough money or high enough test scores can enter its gates; the standards being lowered, of course, to meet the demands of diversity. The quality of the students fails to matter when the professors merely parrot whatever doesn't get them fired. And their precious research?

Most academic publications exist solely to entertain the professors' colleagues and that doesn't seem to be a problem, but woe unto the intrepid voice that speaks to those outside the university's hallowed walls or actually tries to change something within. Anathema!

True academic intellectualism died somewhere in the middle of the twentieth century; it's rotting in a ditch beside the American Dream. Sadly, it was a few decades before we even realized they were missing.

The bottom line is this: Our educators can no longer be trusted. They will not sharpen your mind; do it yourself. He who was once a champion of the freethinker, now forges their chains. Break them. That orator standing in front of the board may have traded his wolf skins for a tweed jacket with suede elbow patches, but you don't have to. If he assigns one text by Camus, read them all. If he tells you not to write so creatively, write a novel. If he tells you to let the department guide your research, cling to your mission with ferocity. Do it your way, inside or outside of that crumbling tower. Wherever your path takes you, stay on it. Walk with abandon, be the brazen voice they whisper about in their hallowed halls.

We needn't care for the opinions of our universities for they are no longer citadels of free thinking and revolutionary ideas, but instead places where our best and brightest pay to become programmed links in worldwide chains of technological slavery. The average graduate is just another part of the system, a system that cares not one damn bit for individuals but praises and rewards the collective mentality. These are the places that train our elites and - thanks to intellectual movements infused with cultural Marxism - journalists, lawyers, and economists are churned out on graduation day like assembly line robots ready to engineer society according to their embedded programs.

Go there. Take what you need from that crumbling tower and get out before it collapses. As the dust settles behind you, smile and walk on.

Let Them Eat Cake:

The Inevitable Is Upon Us

Once or twice upon a time, the warrior monks rode out of their citadels of learning to assess the world, talk to the peasant, wallow in the mud and blood with the common man. I dare say they were the better for the experience, as experience is a fine instructor. Today, however, those educated elites instructing young minds have had no experience, for experience reeks of the world outside of the Ivory Tower. They may whisper, *let them eat cake*, as they spurn the world, avoid the masses, and demean those whose worn shoes do not shine. Moreover, within their own walls, souls are crushed for, "elite universities disdain honest intellectual inquiry, which is by its nature distrustful of authority, fiercely independent, and often subversive." *

No, free thought is not wanted in the Tower. Daring and bravery are not wanted. What the string pullers want is for their lauded professors and students alike to retreat into specialized fiefdoms surrounded by walls of impenetrable research. They retreat into these segregated kingdoms of expertise and no longer have anything of worth to say to the world at large. They speak to colleagues. They write for academic journals. They retreat, retreat, retreat; those extra letters after their names tucked away like tails between their untried legs.

Those legs are more often than not hidden under a desk mere feet from bookshelves lined with the thoughts of others. Here they write in a language that cares not one bit for universal understanding or appeal; picking and choosing from a list of obscure words that obfuscate communication altogether, and deliberately so. The illusion of profundity is created and thus the uninitiated ask no questions and propose no objections as the initiated blindly carry on, ignoring the larger moral and social issues boiling over just outside their ivory walls. When the moat is awash in blood, eating away at the foundations of their citadel, it will not stand. The fires of discontent are spreading, the smoke is thickening, and a pile of bodies has made a bridge to an untended gate. Will those inside join the battle?

I challenge our great thinkers to join the fray, to preserve the very culture they purport to teach, to pick up both pen and sword and come out of hiding. While these bright minds have indeed painted themselves into very prestigious corners, the time has come for the brave amongst them to brazenly walk out of the Tower or turn 'round and tear down the walls, laughing as the dust settles behind them. The alternative? Crushed in the rubble of their own fallen kingdom. Know this: it will fall. The inevitable is upon us and a decision must be made. Choose your weapon.

*Hedges, Chris. The Empire of Illusion: The End Of Literacy and the Triumph of Spectacle. NY, NY: Nation Books, 2010, p. 89.

The Years of Decay

Modern University or Citadel of Nonsense

Allow me to paint for you, dear reader, a picture: A middle-aged women to whom time has not been kind. She is spindly limbed, pot-bellied, and lean-lipped with thinning, wispy hair dyed a different color every other week. No discernible jaw line or chin, slouching narrow shoulders, a permanent frown. Folded down wool socks crammed into ill-fitting sandals underneath a mismatched attempt at bohemian attire gone horribly awry.

She says, "What's that book about?"

"The decline of academia," I answer.

She scowls, pouts, and replies, "Well, I'm a college professor…"

Bear with me as I try not to laugh then explain, "It touches on the unnecessary scholarship pushed by a lot of institutions these days."
Her face scrunches and contorts as she spits out, "There's no such thing as unnecessary scholarship."

At this point, I'm no longer trying not to laugh. Standing in front of a computer, I silently but with a smirk type in "ridiculous academic research" and 6,860,000 results pop up immediately. I walk away. Academics have been deliberately dumbing down society for decades now and this professor is just another victim trained to perpetuate the system. So self-assured in her intellect, it might crush her to realize that grading freshmen composition papers at a state school known more for its alcoholism than its academics is not impressive. No, adjunct professor of formulaic prose, you are not impressive in the least.

And the Ivory Tower is no longer imposing, not when countless hours and dollars are spent analyzing the color of benches in a particular shopping mall, which research is then discussed ad nauseam and with all seriousness. This is mental masturbation, nothing more. What about this or that pop stars choice of attire? Perhaps her sequined nipples represent something hidden deep in society's underbelly? Let's apply for a grant to get to the bottom of this! Russell Jacoby said it best, "The problem is not the determination to take popular culture seriously…rather it is the failure to say anything illuminating."*

 Sadly, illumination is no longer the focus of most academics for that would cause the tenure-tracked intellectual to stand out whereas the goal in today's universities is to fit in, toe the line, and never – ever – strive to stand taller than the other professor poppies by publishing anything that might shake the foundations of that crumbling Ivory Tower, so near to collapse.

*Jacoby, Russell. *The End of Utopia*. New York, NY: Basic Books, 1999, p. 81.

Government and Finance

Tar and Taxes

"Single acts of tyranny may be ascribed to the accidental opinion of a day; but a series of oppressions, begun at a distinguished period, and pursued unalterably through every change of ministers, too plainly prove a deliberate
systematical plan of reducing us to slavery."

~Thomas Jefferson

I thought about our rebels' roots; everything has roots. Who were our first rebels? I guess we all were to some extent here in America, at least the ones who came willingly. Those who fought against the British were surely rebels. More significantly, they were farmers. After they won the war, they went back to their farms only to be taxed by their own government more than they'd ever been by the Crown; someone had to pay for the war, after all. What were they taxing? Whiskey. And so we have Whiskey Rebellion.

Corn was a cash crop for these farmers, and making whisky out of it was far more profitable than a tasty cob here and there. Thus whiskey was taxed to the point that many a whiskey rebel went right out of business, legally speaking. The percolating stills simply went into hiding and the guns came out. In 1794, the Whisky Rebels were crushed and thus began American taxation on this, that, and the other. This out of control taxation continues even today, and it has only gotten worse since the Federal Reserve Act and its partner, the Internal Revenue Service, were signed into action.

A little here, a little there, and now the average citizen can't even collect his own rain water. Just yesterday I skimmed over an online article claiming that the government owns the wind, thereby shutting down renewable wind-based power plants.

Is this really happening? Is this why those farmers volunteered to fight the British? Clearly, something has gone terribly wrong. We are taxed on damn near everything, again and again, and the tax rates continue to climb while the value of the dollar continues to drop. It was not like this before 1913, and still we had roads, schools, and courthouses. So, why do we need the Federal Reserve and the IRS? The answer is We the People do NOT need the IRS or the Federal Reserve. They need us.

They need us, and our compliance, simply to exist. When one considers the fact – yes, fact – that these shady institutions are unconstitutional, one wonders why we tolerate this at all. I would insert a link here, but a simple internet search yields hundreds of results, including the IRS' refutation worded in consummate legalese enough to break the resolve of anyone who might rebel, whiskey or not. Others refuse the refutations. Nonetheless, the Sixteenth Amendment seems clear enough - ***the IRS should not exist***.

What would the Whiskey Rebels do in light of this questionable fleecing? They might start with a shot…of whiskey, that is. Then? In the 1790's most simply refused to pay, others threatened the tax officer himself with violence. This usually amounted to nothing more than not allowing him to set up an office in their town, but sometimes a particularly stubborn tax collector would be tarred and feathered. In one town in Pennsylvania, there was a shootout between the townsfolk, the tax collector, and his slaves (yes, there were slaves in Pennsylvania). Finally, in 1794, George Washington called together a militia and marched toward the rebels' strongholds. Several were arrested, though none were prosecuted. The notorious tax lived on.

We might call that the start of a downward spiral that gained tremendous momentum in 1913 with the passing of the Federal Reserve Act and the IRS. Today, we seem to be spiraling out of control. Tarring and feathering the folks at the local IRS office will likely not help matters, but it's a start.

For the curious: http://www.activistpost.com/2016/08/state-now-claims-owns-wind-taxing-renewable-energy-existence.html

Free Trade Is Not Free

Until World War II, a mere two percent of the United States' economy was dependent on foreign trade. Now? Now it is hard to find even an American flag that is not made in China. Why? It wasn't economic necessity but the result of deliberate and calculated manipulation. Indeed, since our grandparents stumbled back from Europe's bloodied shores, our economy has been steadily passed from American to foreign hands.

1947 saw the beginning of this transfer. This was the year the United Nations affected the GATT treaty. GATT, or the General Agreement on Tariffs and Trade, was passed at a UN meeting in Geneva and the American economy has slowly crumbled since. If we are not making or purchasing products made in this country, we are hurting our economy. It is that simple. Also, trading with countries who pile up labor violations does no one any good. This is not "free" trade but an encouragement to those who would enact slave labor.

The Council on Foreign Relations adores the idea of "free" trade. Free to whom is the question we should ask, as well as the Council on what? Who are these people? They are, by and large, career politicians and the international bankers who control them. Even Hillary Clinton made a(nother) faux pas when she publicly admitted that it would be nice having a new CFR headquarters so close by to tell her what to do. No, she was not being facetious. There are hundreds of recordings of this.

The CFR goes back several decades and as their power grew, the power of the American economy and the living standards of the average citizen declined. Such an inverse relationship begs investigation. As for the question of "free" to whom, the answer is no less murky. Free trade means simply no tariffs and no restrictions or quota limits. That means factory workers making pennies on the dollar in Mexico can sell to American stores an item x for a fraction of the cost that item x costs when made in America. Add to this troubling scenario the fact that many American consumers are often strapped for cash thanks to the IRS and the Federal Reserve's unending inflation, lower wages or even unemployment because of so-called free trade, and higher costs of living in general. The result? Joe and Jane Consumer will buy the cheaper version of item x regardless of where it came from because they can't afford to be patriotic. Not to mention, there is often no option to buy a similar product made in America – not after American factories went overseas for cheaper labor. Plenty of the corporate business owners who decided to move their businesses, by the way, are members of the CFR. The owners' bottom line inflated. The American factory worker was out of a job. So, "free" to whom? Not the average citizen.

Free trade might work to a point between countries of comparable living standards and workplace environments. However, when a country like ours trades with a country like Malaysia where the economy is damn near one of slave labor, no one but the owners of large corporations and their hand-in-hand bankers benefits. Not specific enough? In 2015, Obama let a few things slide in regards to Malaysia and the recent TPP (Trans-Pacific Partnership). Malaysia is notorious for human trafficking, a violation of TPP's standards for participation. That's alright! They have cheap stuff so the deal was signed. Yes, Obama's hope and change did this with nary a word from the mainstream media. Imagine if Trump turned a blind eye to human trafficking in exchange for cheaper goods and a further undermined American economy – the press would never let it go, and they shouldn't regardless of the party in the Oval Office.

The press should dig into this. They should be infuriated. You should be infuriated. As international financiers watch their bottom line expand, our bottom line is this: National sovereignty depends on economic self-sufficiency. We as a nation are no longer self sufficient. The only demographic this benefits is that of the top-tier international financiers and their pocket politicians. Know this: when you hear the innocuous term "free trade" you are hearing something that has cost Americans dearly.

https://www.aei.org/publication/obama-lets-malaysia-off-the-hook-on-human-trafficking-to-achieve-free-trade-deal/

Finance and Control

"The Federal Reserve is an independent agency and that means basically that
there is no other agency of government which can overrule actions that we take."
~ Alan Greenspan, former Chairman of the Federal Reserve

"Let me control the issuance of money in a country and I care not who makes its laws."
~ Mayer Amschel Rothschild

The Federal Reserve issues our currency. No other governmental entity has any control over this monster bank. Thus, it is easy to conclude that maybe, just maybe, those in control of our money supply have an inordinate amount of control over our government as a whole. If one controls the government, one has a high degree of control over the people under its jurisdiction. Are we in conspiracy theory territory? Some will scoff and say yes; I would have just a few years ago. Now I am not so sure, for something is no longer just a theory when it is repeatedly demonstrated. No, at that point the conspiracy theory is an actual conspiracy.

Here come the requisite campaigners to tell us we do have control – we can vote the "bad guy" out of office. What if, dear reader, the bad guy in question was never elected? Whether you screamed *Make America Great Again* or *I'm with Her*, the banking system remained the same – a despotic institution well above the law and well above the electoral process.

Henry Ford told us,

> "It is well enough that the people of the nation do not understand our banking
> and monetary system, for if they did, I believe there would be a revolution before
> tomorrow morning."

Short of a revolution, what can we do if voting is ineffective as many contend? We vote anyway. Imagine this – an outsider so anti-establishment who wins a landslide victory for a prominent, national office. This might strike fear in the hearts of our bankers and they might slip for just a precious second; at the least they would scramble to gain control of this individual. In that second they might drop the proverbial ball. Someone else might pick it up. That is one scenario.

Whether there is an ensuing scramble or not, there is more that We the People can do. I contend that the simplest and quite possibly the most profound thing we can do is NOTHING. That's right, nothing. Not a damn thing. What if, one fateful day, we all simply did nothing? Yes, it's a wild fantasy, but know this – despite this or that legal entity, no one controls you. No one controls any of us. Control is impossible without our consent. We can all get up one day and say NO. Don't go to work. Don't buy anything. Don't even drive. What will our government do? And when those who work for our government also say NO, we've already won. If only the YES men among us said NO, the victory would be absolute.

If it is your job to arrest folks for resisting the government or not paying their bills, do not do your job. If it is your job to garnish folks pay checks because they have loans, do not do your job. If it is your job to collect taxes, do not do your job. If it is your job to evict families, do not do your job. If we all screamed NO by quietly doing nothing, there wouldn't be a damn thing anyone could do about it. On that fine day, the suits inside the Federal Reserve will sit there idly twirling their pens, smugly calling on this or that agency to enact law and order – but no one will answer.

Revolution Calling

"I see in the near future a crisis approaching that unnerves me and causes me to tremble for the safety of my country. Corporations have been enthroned, an era of corruption will follow, and the money power of the country will endeavor to prolong its reign by working on the prejudices of the people, until the wealth is aggregated in a few hands, and the republic destroyed."

By working on the prejudices of the people… This prophetic statement was made on November 21, 1864 by Abraham Lincoln who tried to back out of his banking blunders too late and backed into a bullet. Fast forward to 1913, Jekyll Island Georgia, where wealth [was] aggregated in a few hands and sits there still today. Paul Warburg was at this meeting and he was very soon placed on the board of the brand new Federal Reserve, a position for which he gave up an annual salary at the banking firm of Kuhn, Loeb, & Co. of $500,000 (over ten million dollars today) for the Fed's paltry salary of $12,000. Suspicious? Yes it is; he was NOT a citizen of the United States but a recently imported German/Jewish banker who had no business in the highest echelons of our government – but the Federal Reserve Act was all about business.

Congressman Charles Lindbergh Sr. warned us about this when he said, in 1913, on the floor of the House just before this banking blunder was passed:

"This act establishes the most gigantic trust on earth. When the President signs this act the invisible government by the money power, proven to exist by the money trust investigation, will be legalized."

There it is again, the money power. How does it work? Our befuddled government sells bonds to the bank. The bank gives them money which the government uses to conduct the business of the country. When those bonds mature, the bank cashes them in with interest. The money received by our government from the bank is printed out of thin air. This is fiat currency and it costs the bank nothing. The American tax payer foots the bill, including the accumulated interest.

How can the Feds be sure there will be enough tax dollars? Introduce an income tax. In 1895, the US Supreme Court ruled that an income tax was unconstitutional. That did not stop Nelson Aldrich from introducing a bill calling for an income tax less than twenty years later. Coincidentally, Aldrich was the same Senator who introduced the Federal Reserve bill. On a side note, Aldrich's daughter married a Rockefeller; the Rockefellers, of course, owned plenty of shares in the new Federal Reserve Bank. This is surely just another coincidence.

Here is yet another coincidence: Karl Marx's Communist Manifesto calls for a heavy progressive or graduated income tax and centralization of credit in the hands of the State by means of a national bank with state capital and an exclusive monopoly. Who has a monopoly on our money? The Federal Reserve Bank does, of course. Curiouser and curiouser, as they say.

Enough coincidences. Here is a fact: Our rough and tumble revolutionary ancestors went to war with the British Crown when tax rates reached a puny twenty-one percent. If one combines all of our modern-day taxes – and we are taxed on damn near everything – we are paying a hell of a lot more than twenty-one percent. Forget throwing the tea in the harbor. It is high time our elite Wall Street bankers and their in-pocket politicians got a little wet.

https://www.federalreservehistory.org/people/nelson_w_aldrich
http://laissez-fairerepublic.com/tenplanks.html

Grace Under Fire?

It happened in 1984; perhaps we should have known something was amiss. The report was submitted on January 15, and the results? The money you and I pay in income taxes goes toward paying down the debt to the Federal Reserve while a small percentage is transferred into federal pension plans. In other words, money is siphoned out of our paychecks to enrich bankers and career politicians. That is all. Not one dime is spent on government programs like infrastructure or education. This is surprising, but it should not be when one considers the federal Reserve Act and the income tax laws were passed hand in hand. Or should I say hand in pocket?

The report was filed by the Grace Commission under President Ronald Reagan and the results were only very quietly admitted. One can see why. When a tax payer realizes he or she is paying nothing but debt on fiat currency – paper money with nothing of value behind it aside from your blood, sweat, tears, and years – that tax payer might become disagreeable, to put it mildly. I posit it is high time we become disagreeable.

Why should working Americans pay debt on what amounts to the Emperor's New Clothes? The money is not real! Sure, it is a high quality paper, but that is all it is. The Federal Reserve prints it. We pay exorbitant debt for the privilege of using it. Why should we as a nation not print our own currency as prescribed in the Constitution? This is madness, plain and simple. We are working day afer day to keep the locks on our own asylum.

One could easily label the Internal Revenue Service as the gatekeepers or even the club-wielding guards. What do they do exactly? The IRS is a "Trust" not an agency. This Trust is based out of Puerto Rico where they essentially launder our money and send it hither, thither, and yon; anywhere but back home where it belongs in the pockets of the tax payers whom those friendly agents refer to as inventory. The following sites are agonizing but helpful in figuring all of this out:

http://www.supremelaw.org/sls/31answers.htm
https://www.law.cornell.edu/uscode/text/5/551
https://www.law.cornell.edu/uscode/text/5/552
https://www.law.cornell.edu/uscode/text/18/1951

Matters go from bad to worse when one examines the questionable validity of the Sixteenth Amendment. It seems it was never ratified. And yet, here we go, day after day, whistling while we work to pay taxes that should not exist. Our parents and grandparents did the same, even as the money that came home dwindled while the cost of living crept up. Now, more often than not, both parents work while the children, also dwindling in numbers, are raised by strangers. What does the future hold for our little tax payers, our little bundles of inventory? If we continue on this path, their future is bleak indeed.

What made Reagan open such a contentious can of worms? He knew that We the People were being fleeced and, believe it or not, it seems he actually cared. In May of 1983 he declared,

> "Our federal tax system is, in short, utterly impossible, utterly unjust, and completely counterproductive. [It] reeks with injustice and is fundamentally un-American…it has earned a rebellion and it's time we rebelled."

Reagan was shot on March 30, 1981 and still he criticized the bankers. Is he a hero or does that throw a giant question mark over his findings? One gets the nagging feeling that the Powers That (Should Not) Be want us to rebel, or maybe they just do not care. It makes for a tight narrative if he is shot after his declared findings, but before? The fact that all of this information is fairly easy to find does make one pause for thought. Perhaps our government is simply confident in our complacency. Curiouser and curiouser as we go down the rabbit hole.

I am left wondering, does this stretching hydra that is our government, win either way? Either We the People get angry and rebel, thereby martial law descends and we are further ensnared or we continue behaving as sheep grazing mindlessly to the slaughter. The government wins in both scenarios. What if, dear reader, there is a third option? What if we rebelled and we WON?

Read the report here:
http://thetruthnews.info/GraceCommissionReport.pdfhttp://thetruthnews.info/GraceCommissionReport.pdf

Old Hickory and Old Money

A Case of City Mouse and Country Mouse

Villains. Our history has more of them than our comic books. Why? Question the narrative and you begin to unravel a well-packaged web of lies sold to you by a propaganda machine hell-bent on keeping us all under a barely disguised totalitarian boot. Question the narrative and what you end up with is a mess, not a gleaming and undeniable truth. It's complex and frustrating, but it's not what they told us in history class. It's not what they told us on big screens or small. It's not what they told us in our newspapers and magazines. We were lied to, and that is the first and most important truth to which we must cling. The rest of the intricate mess will unravel in time if we stop believing the lies.

I've just seen a few minutes of the evening news. It seems they're still throwing around the idea of removing Jackson from the twenty dollar bill and replacing him with Harriet Tubman. Anyone who knows the history of the banks knows why, and it has nothing to do with honoring Tubman. No, that's just empty appeasement. Jackson didn't want a central bank, so why would they want him on their currency? It was nothing but a smug slap in Jackson's weathered face and a smug reminder to those who'd fight the bank today - you'll lose.

Of course, the shady history of the banking cartel was never mentioned by the perky newscaster. Instead, it was the trite but effective Jackson was cruel to the Cherokee and Tubman rescued slaves! As if that's all we remember. Some of us remember more, so much more. Old Hickory didn't just fight the Cherokee - which must be judged in context - he also fought the Bank of the United States, the forerunner to the Federal Reserve, in the person of Nicholas Biddle in a confrontation fit for any tall tale. Jackson was a roughened man from the frontier, a simple but stern fellow from the country, while Biddle was what Jackson's neighbors' would call one of them fancy city folk, wealthy and refined. They first clashed in 1832, a re-election year. The bank's charter was good for four more years, but Biddle shrewdly petitioned for early renewal thinking Jackson wouldn't stir the pot too much during an election year; he was wrong. Jackson vetoed his appeal for renewal and all hell broke loose.

Biddle used his pull with Congress (pull meaning he was giving them pay-offs) to offset the President and they ate up his offerings like pigs at a trough. While Biddle pulled government strings, Jackson pulled the heartstrings of the citizens. He won the election and promptly saw to it that all new federal deposits went to state banks, not the central bank. No, the central bank was used to pay expenses. Jackson wanted to empty Biddle's accounts, of course, but the shrewd banker countered by contracting the money supply and ceasing all loans. Economic hardship ensued and Jackson was blamed, for a time.

The fancy fellow from the city was just too full of himself, however, and was overheard one too many times boasting of how he'd broken the economy and the President as well. Public opinion turned. Jackson was cut from a different cloth, more like the citizens. As this played out in front of the nation, the governor of Pennsylvania, where Biddle was from, publicly denounced the bank and its director. That was it. A committee was formed to investigate both Biddle and the bank but he flatly refused to cooperate. Congress was at a loss; if they pressed on he could blackmail all of them.

No matter, at this point Jackson had succeeded in paying off the national debt and had even stacked up a surplus which he then gave back to the states. That's when the bullets started flying, though Jackson was spared thanks to a misfire. It was 1835 and the would-be assassin was found not guilty due to insanity, only to be later witnessed bragging about the wealthy and powerful Europeans who were protecting him thus confirming Jackson's complaint that the bank was unduly influenced by foreign interests. Clearly, Jackson had won. By 1836, the charter for the Bank of the United States expired and Biddle was finally arrested and charged with fraud.*

Yes, it's a hell of a story, and only part of the legacy of Old Hickory. He also expanded the power of the federal government and the executive office to points from which they have unfortunately never returned. He did this by sheer force of character, and that is the kind of soul it takes to fight the entrenched banking cartel. We need another such soul, one with iron sides. Like Old Hickory, this warrior will have a tainted past and an unmatched ego, but what else can slay monsters?

*For a thorough but manageable account of Jackson and the Bank of the United States, see G. Edward Griffin's *The Creature from Jekyll Island: A Second Look at the Federal Reserve*.

Chess Anyone?

International Intrigues and the Federal Reserve

When one studies the early years of the Federal Reserve, one name stands out again and again, that of Warburg. Who is this powerful and German-Jewish family and why did they have so much influence in our government and over our finances?

Shortly after the Federal Reserve Act was passed, on Christmas Eve in 1913, the enormously influential German banking firm of Kuhn, Loeb & Co. sent one of their senior partners back to the United States to run the Fed - that's right, from its start the Fed was in the hands of a foreigner, one Paul Moritz Warburg.

Why? The why of it all would lead us down a cumbersome and lengthy digression the length of a Russian novel, but Russia does enter into this story. A short digression about the nature of Warburg's business is necessary for at least a cursory understanding of the nature of our problem; our problem being the beast known as the Fed, or more properly the Federal Reserve. So, Kuhn, Loeb & Co? It was an international banking firm that financed the Russian Revolution, placing the bloody Bolsheviks firmly in power. It was Jacob Schiff, Kuhn Loeb's front man in New York and brother-in-law to Mr. Warburg, who paved the way for Leon

Trostsky to slip smoothly into Russia, going so far as to convince the President to give the criminal a passport. This does not even scratch the surface of their political intrigues, and yet we see that these Warburgs and their ilk can and do play chess with the world as their board.

The American people didn't want to play. In fact, we wanted nothing to do with a Central Bank, and yet Paul Warburg did a fine job of making the Fed appear magnanimous to the average voter. He didn't call it a bank and there was to be more than one major branch, thereby allaying suspicions of central control. It was all a show and we fell for it. Why were the high-powered bankers themselves calling for banking reform, reform they intended to handle? It seems we didn't ask as Warburg traveled the states convincing the public that reform was crucial for a stable economic future.* He didn't mention the new income tax that would go along with it, a tax that would pay our government's debt to these bankers who were so kind as to print our money for us and loan it to the treasury at interest, the interest coming out of our paychecks, naturally. No, this absurdity wasn't mentioned. Stability, predictability, and growth! That was mentioned ad nauseam.

The machinations continued into the next generation. Paul's son and the nephew of Jacob Schiff, was a Mr. James Paul Warburg, another big shot for Kuhn Loeb & Co. On February 17, 1950, this lovely fellow said to the US Senate, "We shall have World Government, whether or not we like it. The only question is whether World Government will be achieved by conquest or consent." James, too, was foreign born. He was introduced to the Fed via Roosevelt himself who, after seizing the nation's gold supply in 1933, deposited this younger Warburg into the Treasury, where he had his own room - one needs a room of one's own when involved in international intrigues, of course.

Yes, this foreign-born Mr. Warburg stayed inside the United States Treasury and visited its offices daily. Oh, that's not the least bit suspicious, or is it? It's difficult to keep this brief, but you get the idea. The Untied States Federal Reserve is a key piece on the chess board of international finance, and we are the tax-paying pawns.

As I write this, it's mid-April and your taxes are due…again. Remember this: If you get a refund, that isn't the government being generous. That was your money to begin with and the Feds should never have taken it. If you're paying even more than you've already paid, ask your local IRS agent just where that money goes. The IRS, by the way, is based not out of this country but out of Puerto Rico.** That is a story for another day.

*Griffin, G. Edward. *The Creature from Jekyll Island: A Second Look at the Federal Reserve* (Fifth Edition). American Media, 2010, p. 444.

** This alarming fact is readily available via multiple sources. A simple internet search (IRS headquarters Puerto Rico) yields plenty of results.

Pounds and Pennies:

Ezra Pound and Our Corrupt Financial System

He suffered because he knew; he knew and he told us. Who was Ezra Pound? He was a poet who saw through the facade of central banking and chastised not only elite financiers but also the American people for allowing themselves to lose control over their own money. We were lazy. We let ourselves be duped, and we have not changed except to slip further into economic amnesia. It is time to shake it off.

The fog started to settle during the Civil War. Before that, nationally issued and controlled money was the standard, culminating in Lincoln's greenbacks. These bills were short-lived however, because Lincoln let the bankers in the back door with the National Banking Act; he had to win the war, after all, and the South and all her money had to be kept under a federal boot. Lincoln soon regretted the banking act and aimed at limiting the financiers' power. They aimed a gun at his head. We know who fired first.

In 1913, the bankers' grip on this country was further tightened with the Federal Reserve Act and we've been in their noose ever since. Ezra wanted to know, what is money for and how did this absurd paper money become so damned important? Smoke and mirrors was essentially his answer. Quite simply, we've been fooled. Those who control the flow of currency control the nation by contracting or expanding the money supply, thereby playing with inflation, employment, private ownership, supply and demand, all aspects of our economy. Pound saw no reason our nation couldn't control the flow of its own currency, as provided for in our own Constitution. Why do we need these middle-men bankers? We don't. We don't need them for a damned thing.

What an inconvenient answer. Pound told it like it was. He declared, "The usurers act through fraud, falsification, superstitions, habits and, when these methods do not function, they let loose a war…"

He was right and due to his opinionated radio broadcasts from fascist Italy, Franklin Roosevelt had him arrested for treason and imprisoned in an asylum for twelve years. Thou shalt not speak ill of thine bankers.

What did the poet say that was treasonous? Nothing. Pound called for a return to the Constitutionally granted power of printing and regulating our own money, per article one section eight. The fact that we don't do so is patently absurd and the interest we pay to use the Federal Reserve's bank notes is ruining this country.

We can and we must dig ourselves out of this mess. The Federal Reserve can and must be abolished. We absolutely can and must print and regulate our own currency as proscribed in our own Constitution. We seem to have forgotten these freedoms and abilities; it's time to remember. There is not time like the present to shake off our collective amnesia and remember who We the People are. Our founding fathers gave us the tools to create and manage a prosperous economy;

we can and must pick up those tools and use them. But first, the torch and pitchfork - we can and must run the bankers out of Washington.

The Money Changers:

The McFadden Speech and the Corruption of the Federal Reserve

Two shots were fired at him, but they lodged in the metal of the taxi doors. Poison was mixed into his meal, but his stomach was pumped just in time. Finally, three years after the groundbreaking speech that placed a target on his head, he died most unexpectedly after a "dose" of intestinal flu and sudden heart failure. Another round of poisoning? Perhaps. Congressman Louis T. McFadden is gone, but his speech remains and it is just as powerful as it ever was.

The date was May 23, 1933. The place was the floor of the House of Representatives, where McFadden gave a lengthy and detailed speech about the abuses and crimes of the Board of Governors of the Federal Reserve Bank, the Comptroller of the Currency, and the Secretary of the Treasury. The charges included conspiracy, fraud, and treason. The judiciary committee received his articles for impeachment, but did nothing. Given what soon happened to McFadden, it is no great mystery why.

McFadden did not mince words. He began by announcing, "We have in this country one of the most corrupt institutions the world has ever known. I refer to the Federal Reserve Board and the Federal Reserve Banks."

He went on to call them "moneyed vultures," who "created a reign of terror in Russia with our money" by instigating the Russian (Bolshevik) Revolution. He accuses former President Wilson of establishing a bank that now controls us "from the top down, from the cradle to the grave." He asserts that this bank "fastened down upon the country the very tyranny from which the framers of the Constitution sought to save us."*

Do his charges have any merit? It is no secret that the value of the dollar has plummeted since the Fed was instituted. It is no secret that America was doing just fine before the implementation of the income tax, which pays nothing but our debt to the Federal Reserve (see Reagan's Grace Commission report)** . It is likewise no secret that politicians who openly challenge this bank find themselves on the wrong side of a gun; e.g. Lincoln and Jackson to name only two. A corrupt institution? Yes, I'd say that's a fair charge.

This bank has complete control over our money supply and creates as much or as little as it pleases out of nothing. According to our Constitution, this sort of unchecked power has no place in this country. Often, the Fed uses this unprecedented power to flood the market with currency which only debases the value, hence the dollar's ninety-five percent loss in worth since 1913. Further, the Fed is run by folks you and I likely will not recognize. These people are not elected and they answer to no one. What they do is create false booms and busts that wreak havoc in our economy. We can't investigate, of course, for the Fed is not subject to audit. Thus, they give money to whomever they please as they did in 2008, when I was looking at foreclosure papers even as a long list of foreign banks were receiving stacks of our money.*** A corrupt institution? Yes, I'd say that's a fair charge.

I could list pages of charges, but McFadden has already done that; read his speech. In it is a prescient warning about this so-called bank. Andrew Jackson warned us as well. So did Abraham Lincoln and many others, like Henry Cabot Lodge who, one week before the passing of the Federal Reserve Act, wrote a letter to fellow senator Weeks in which he predicted that the Fed would "open the way to a vast inflation of the currency," and would "harm the general welfare of the people of the United States."

Lodge was right. This Federal Reserve Bank has done infinitely more harm than good and will continue to do so as long as We the People allow it to operate. We must remember front-line soldiers like McFadden, Jackson, and Lincoln who directly attacked this monster. We need courageous men like this to face the beast head on whilst countless other brave souls flank its sides and take it down. Won't you join us? Won't you help us make McFadden's prophecy come true?

> "I predict that the American people, outraged, pillaged, insulted, and betrayed as they are in their own land, will rise up in their wrath, and will sweep the money changers out of the temple."
>
> ~ Louis T. McFadden

*http://libertyforlife.com/banking/us-mcfadden-re-frb.htm
**https://www.alipac.us/f19/grace-commission-report-under-ronald-reagan-showed-irs-103958/
***http://www.freedomworks.org/content/top-10-reasons-end-federal-reserve

The Sixteenth Amendment:

A Question of Legitimacy

Christmas Eve, 1913. The United States Congress. An amendment was pushed through when few if any were paying attention. From that day forward, Americans have been paying an income tax that may or may not have been legitimately ratified. Moreover, the United States had paved roads, public schools, and a workable sense of law and order before the income tax, which begs the question: What exactly are we paying for? According to President Reagan's Blue Ribbon Panel Grace Commission,

> "One hundred percent of what is collected is absorbed solely by interest on the federal debt. All individual income tax revenues are gone before one nickel is spent on the services taxpayers expect from government."

What we are paying for, then, is the government's debt to the federal reserve which prints and distributes the money and charges our government – us – interest for so doing. Questions abound. Why does our government not print its own money? They certainly have the power to do so. Further, was the amendment even properly ratified or is it unconstitutional? There are serious defects in the ratification process of this amendment; enough to cast doubt on its legitimacy. Typographical errors alone would have been enough to make the process null and void.*

For the sake of argument, let's say it was ratified with no problems. Now turn to Article One, Section Nine of the Constitution and note that it is, in fact, unconstitutional to tax citizens directly on their property, wages, salaries, or earnings. Moreover, Supreme Court judges have repeatedly rejected claims that the amendment actually amended the constitution in regards to limits on direct taxation.**

We are on unstable ground to say the least, but tax day finds us year after year - and red and yellow, black and white had better fill out those aggravating forms. When you do, remember this: The day the Sixteenth Amendment was passed is the day we all became debt slaves; some are simply more clever at padding the chains and avoiding the whip though we all remain in servitude. If it's equality you want, thank the bankers for making it possible. We are all owned, from the day we are born, in equal shares by our government which in turn is owned by the bankers who print our meaningless money. There's your equality; isn't it grand? I recently overheard a day-dreaming liberal muse, anything that moves us closer to equality is good. Anything? I urge you, be careful what you wish for.

*See Document no. 97-120 of the 97th Congress, First Session, entitled How Our Laws Are Made, written by Edward F. Willet, Jr. Esq.
**For an example, see Brushaber vs. Union Pacific.

The Power of Illusion:

The Madness of Civilization Is In Your Pocket

"When a government is dependent on bankers for money, they and not the leaders of the government control the situation, since the hands that gives is above the hand that takes…Money has no mother land; financiers are without patriotism and without decency; their sole object is gain."

~ Napoleon Bonaparte

Money. We are here solely to churn the fake money. Of course it all means nothing in this modern economy, just numbers on a screen, but oh the power of numbers! These are the hours you'll spend toiling away, time forever lost and never enough numbers on your side of the screen, not when the commas and zeroes are reserved for those who hold the keys to the vaults. The banks own you. They own your house, your car, your future, your government, your country, your world. Banks are the temples of modernity. One must worship on their steps if one wishes to receive any blessings, for these brick and mortar edifices hold more power than ever did the greatest of kingdoms or the Holy See.

I walked past one of these citadels just last week and stopped to look at the stark architecture. A homeless man approached me and said, "Stay away from that place. It's not what you think." Curious, I asked him to tell me what it meant to him. His reply, below, was more insightful than I expected:

"I'll tell you what that building means. It's about this - this civilization, or whatever you wanna call it. Y'all is crazy. You spend all day, day after day, going from one damn box to another. You wake up in a big box called home. That box costs you most of the money you make when you go to the box called work. You spend all day there and ain't got no time to spend in the house box you're paying so much for. And how'd you get back and forth? You pay for another little box, this one on wheels that you gotta pay to replace cause you wear 'em out all the damn time running between boxes. Then you gotta pay more money just to make it move. Then you gotta pay even more money for permission to drive it on roads that you already done paid for before you even get your damn check. What the hell is wrong with y'all? You know where that money comes from, don't you? Nowhere. They done made it up outta air but you gotta trade in your life for it. Yeah, pretty girl, I call y'all crazy. And you call me crazy cause I don't want nothing to do with it. Now ain't humanity a joke?"

My simple reply was, "Yes, sir, it is. Thank you for reminding me." He's right, of course. Inside that imposing granite edifice are the pens, papers, and screens that make money out of absolutely nothing, and yet we kill for it. Stark, raving madness indeed.

Minted Monopoly Money

Dealer, Please Give Me Another

"The modern banking process manufactures currency out of nothing.
The process is perhaps the most astounding piece of sleight of hand
that was ever invented… If you want to be slaves of the bankers, and
pay the cost of your own slavery, then let the banks create currency."

~ Lord Josiah Stemp, Former Director of the Bank of England (1937)

Everything seems to be about money these days. And what exactly is money? Since 1913, it has become a largely intangible or even abstract idea. In large part, it doesn't even exist. Nonetheless, what it means to the banks and the government is power - and they get it by inventing it from thin air. No actual wealth need be involved. Their guarantee in its value is you - your sweat, blood, tears, and years. Your life; that's what it means to you. You work day after day after day to get those dollars but it will likely never be enough. The banks and the government get it by typing in a few extra numbers on a screen. It doesn't necessarily have to be printed on paper anymore. What a wonder - the emperor's new clothes do exist!

None of this is taught in schools, but let's say you decide go to school anyway. You're going to need money, so you get a quick and easy student loan. Very well, buttons are pushed and numbers on one screen are simply transferred to another screen. If there's any of those magic numbers left after tuition, they hand you a piece of paper that you put in your bank and voila! more numbers on yet another screen. Maybe you get cash, but probably not. No matter, it's worthless just the same, until they want their "money" back. And then? Those numbers that cost them absolutely nothing will cost you thirty years. Work, work, work, and you might make a dent. Oh, and they'll want back four or five times what you actually borrowed. It means nothing to them, everything to you.

For the feds, it's just an electronic transfer of fiat funds forcibly taken from the tax payer to begin with; the portion of the alleged money that actually exists, that is. For you, it's a lower standard of living, going without, time forever lost. Congratulations, you have earned a degree and an indentured servitude! Of course, no one knows that when they sign the cursed papers. No college freshman thinks he won't get a good job and pay off those loans with ease as soon as he has that coveted degree. Unfortunately, it doesn't work that way for most of us. By the time the wayward graduate figures that out, the shackles are on. Those momentary numbers on a glowing screen will cost you everything. I can't help but feel like the American Dream is dead and I tripped over the corpse during my graduation.

A large portion of our lives, debt or no debt, is dedicated to that intangible thing we call money. It's fiat currency. It doesn't exist, yet you can't live without it! Try it. Go off the grid, install a few solar panels on a house you built, grow your own food. You might get away with it, or you might go to jail on a domestic terrorism charge. No bombs need be involved, just a barrel for catching rain water will suffice. In other words, you are a servant to the state; we all are. Should you refuse that servitude, you are an extremist and you will be treated accordingly. We are teetering on the brink of totalitarianism and more promises by more government will push us over the edge. *But their social programs sound so noble!* Whine, whine, whine the swine who argue that if a politician wants to structure the government so that it gives back, why shouldn't we let him?

Because the government has nothing to give. NOTHING.

Nothing, that is, without taxing you, me, and everyone else into a newly defined poverty - let's call it a classless society; that sounds nice. And so, in time, we will all become equals; all except those with the power to transfer numbers and commas from one screen to another, those with the power to hire guns after they've taken ours away, those we think we've elected as well as the handful of banking cartels who staged the election. The rest of us, the 99.9%, well, we've been given the gift of equality. Isn't it wonderful! An idealists' dream come true, we are, thanks to one magnanimous government program after another, all equals on the bottom rung. The middle, by this time, is empty and the flower of socialism has bloomed into tyranny. Such are the seeds we are planting.

Do we sit back while the idealists among us continue digging their garden? Go on, let's watch them dig deep enough to bury the bloated corpse that is the American dream. It died when Woodrow Wilson was in office and I'm not sure we can bring it back.

The solution? Dream another dream, but I suppose that's easier said than done in a society that puts a price on everything and recognizes the true worth of absolutely nothing. Meanwhile, we have become perpetual consumers who blame the corporations for our woes because the media tells us to even as we scream for more, more, more. We should be screaming no, no, no, even if it starts as a whisper. Stop buying the latest gadgets. Stop getting loans for grossly overpriced cars and oversized houses. Stop buying clothes because of the name on the god damn label.

Even if you manage to avoid blatant consumerism, the banks win whether you succeed or not. That's our real problem, and I don't mean the suit who cashes your checks. I mean the puppeteer who owns not just the corner branch but the whole damn tree. It is they who killed the American Dream with their debt-based economy, income tax, and interest on top of interest on top of interest.

It was Jekyll Island, 1913, but nobody knew for decades what we'd gotten into and sadly most people still don't get it. Even if they do, they're comfortable enough and don't want to risk the status quo. It's too easy to look the other way and too damn dangerous to directly challenge the system - or such is the confidence of the powers that be. Their confidence is so high, in fact, that one may be able to sneak in underneath, unnoticed, and bring it all down.

With a Rebel Yell

With a Rebel Yell, we cried Moore, Moore, Moore. We did not yell loud enough, nor did the GOP who all but abandoned the candidate, nor did Roy Moore himself who was essentially lazy about the whole campaign. Moore lost for a number of reasons, some of them baffling. For instance, the media smear stuck despite the age of the alleged "pedophilia" incident and the admittedly falsified nature of the claims.* This factor is likely a case of media blitz overriding common sense. Perhaps Moore simply was not well liked. Perhaps his campaign was lax. Whatever the case, he lost for any number of reasons, and the underlying issues are perhaps more important than the finer points of the election process.

In a Tweet by one Noah Berlatsky from December 12, 2017, at 7:37 p.m., we read, "black people are turning out in higher numbers than 2014. white turnout it down. the problem here, as everywhere in america, is that there still may be too many white people." [sic]

The errors belong to Mr. Berlatsky, as does the sentiment. Too many white people? Insert any other race into that statement and Mr. Berlatsky might lose his beloved blue check mark. Twitter, however, does not censor racism against whites. This is but one minor incidence of the racial divide that clearly affected the outcome of this election.

Racial fault lines, however, were not the only flaws here. Nonetheless, the suspect power of the polls has spoken and those fault lines were evident. And yet what really happened at the polls? There are now multiple admissions of voter fraud. People came from all over the country to vote, as one newscaster reported. One man admits to voting several times. Thousands of felons were registered at the last minute. Ads were placed in neighboring states for democratic voters to make a short trip to Alabama. Unbelievable? A quick YouTube search yields the interview footage – which I would also deem suspect as no one in his or her right mind would admit to these things on camera. Still, it is possible. It is even likely that fraud occurred, as it regularly does. A larger issue and one that should be looked into is this: it was ruled that the contentious election results can lawfully and immediately be destroyed.** Why would any legitimate voting results in such a notable election not be put on full display if only to quiet dissenters? Even requesting that the results be destroyed stinks to a proverbial high heaven.

At this point, the law abiding citizen throws up his hands and may even give up on voting. Corruption is present in any election, as ubiquitous as cameras are at the polling stations. Those cameras recording one voter after another showing up in the preferred candidates paraphernalia, let's say three to one over another candidate, makes it damn near impossible to commit blatant fraud. More importantly, not voting – unless it is an obvious protest by ALL of a particular group – is an admission of defeat. Why give the other candidate an easy victory? What will you do afterwards? Our election system is far from perfect, with our choices often reduced to the lesser of two evils, but it is a way to be heard just the same. A few votes is but a whisper, a landslide is a veritable rebel yell in some cases, and one very hard to silence.

Would Moore's victory have been such a yell or would he have only been a liability? Opinions are divided on the issue, but he lost regardless. Will there be an investigation? There are a number of factors that do warrant a closer look. What comes next is anyone's guess. Outcomes aside, there is a lesson to be learned here. Run a tight and tireless campaign. Throw back everything a corrupted media throws at you. Have all voters record their time in the polling booth. If your opponent has a weak spot, hit it again and again. In this case, if your opponent is outspending you to an outrageous degree when his voters are among the poorest of the poor, let them know. Moore failed to do this. Moore failed in many ways. May we learn from this failure and move on to bigger and better things.

*http://www.breitbart.com/big-government/2017/12/08/bombshell-roy-moore-accuser-admits-forged-yearbook/

**http://www.al.com/news/index.ssf/2017/12/in_final-hour_order_court_rule.html

Immigration and the Multi-Cult

And the Warriors Will March On

We have all heard it: America is a nation of immigrants and we should accept more immigrants! The charge is foolish at best. This country was not originally a nation of immigrants; it wasn't even a country but a land mass with no established governmental entity to be an immigrant unto. No, our first Americans were not immigrants. They were explorers, conquerors, pioneers, and settlers. It was they who made immigration possible.

Still, the "nation of immigrants" charge has become a veritable mantra of the left. I wonder, would they have said that to the Cherokee? They were the principle tribe in the area where I live now and they were not here first. No, they displaced other tribes and often brutally so. On one mountain in north Georgia - Fort Mountain - local legend (recorded by an anthropologist in the eighteenth century as well as other sources) tells us that a mysterious group of light-haired and "moon-eyed" whites lived there until the Cherokee began to settle the area and then? The Cherokee removed them, got rid of them, drove them off the land; pick a euphemism. Other tribes were "replaced" as well. So much for diversity.*

Gradually, the conquering tribes found themselves on the defensive rather than the offensive side of the land grab, and defend they did. The bottom line is this: if the indigenous populations who preceded European settlers had had the wherewithal and the resources to successfully resist the white man's encroachment on their lands, they certainly would have done so. As it is, they put up a ferocious fight and very nearly won; for this they deserve our eternal respect. Still, they lost. At least this was a declared battle; one knew one's enemy and was not shamed into simply accepting defeat.

What is happening now is entirely different. And if it wasn't? SO WHAT. Everyone has the right to resist invasion, to resist the removal of their culture, to resist the replacement or even extinction of their race. Indeed, every race has the right to protect itself by any means necessary. Waving a flag of virtue within sight of the native will do neither race any good. If they were allowed to defend themselves - and I've heard no warriors for social justice decry a single scalping or settlement burning - we too can defend ourselves. At the least, the white man was forthright in his intention. He did not arrive looking to be coddled while promising to assimilate. No, he stepped off the boat with gun in hand and planted a flag. Though friendships and alliances were undoubtedly made, and broken, the lines between red and white were clear. In this underhanded, scheming mess we see today, the battle has not even been declared and those who would exterminate the white man go on pretending that any who smell smoke are imagining things.

Those of us paying attention smell smoke. We see flames. We will not be shamed into silence. Like those who preceded us, we will put up one hell of a fight. Some of those who met us here centuries ago stalked these woods with belts of dripping scalps, necklaces of severed ears, blades in hand. Should they apologize? Hell no! They should remind the weak-kneed tolerance babblers that they were not simply trading turquoise beads and smoking peace pipes when whitey landed – to pretend they were victims and nothing more is an insult to their warriors' souls. These proud folk defended their land, their way of life, and their race. Why should today's Americans do any less?

To capitulate to invasion is not just cowardice, it is madness. To accept with open arms those huddled masses who arrive with one hand out for alms while the other hand clutches a knife under a hijab is not just naivety, *it is suicide*. Should a social justice warrior crawl out from under the rats in the woodpile and throw down on your path an illusive moral imperative to tolerate, accept, even embrace a so-called immigrant, simply step over their nonsense and march on. The battle is not on the horizon. It is here.

* https://www.legendsofamerica.com/ga-fortmountain/

Do Not Wail At My Wall

The suicide of the West continues. One thing common to so many of the suicide notes, i.e. the pathologically altruistic behavior of Europe's citizens and leaders, is this: they compare the refugees' situation to that of Jews fleeing persecution in Hitler's Germany. Here we go! Everything is Hitler's fault, even still. This fluffy, white blanket of guilt has been stretched to the ripping point, however, and the careful observer can see through it. What do we see? *Nothing*. There is nothing there. The comparisons are faulty and feeble. Still, most will lap up the white guilt. *Never forget*! They scream.

Cecilia Wikström, a member of the European Parliament for the center-right Liberal Party, has pushed the Holocaust on her fellow Swedes as a point of ridiculous reference regarding migrants. She complains that Europe as a whole is not doing enough to help refugees arrive safely and that (oh the horror!) future generations may compare their inactivity to Europe's ignoring the Holocaust. She said,

> "I think that my children and grandchildren are going to ask why more wasn't done to help people running away from Isis, or violence in Eritrea or wherever, when we knew that people were dying in their thousands. People will ask the same question they did

after the war,'if you were aware, why didn't you do something?'. In Sweden we allowed our railroads to be used to transfer Jews to Nazi death camps."*

Cecilia, your children and grandchildren may never see the light of the day. If they do, they will likely be a persecuted minority or they will be Muslims of mixed heritage. They will not ask you why you did not help the downtrodden refugee, but they may well ask why their grandparents were so foolish, naive, and suicidally altruistic as to allow their own kith and kin to be displaced in their own hereditary lands. Cecilia, if your granddaughter is forced into a burka and married the second she reaches puberty, if not before, she may ask why you betrayed her. Cecilia, what will you say to that little girl when Sweden is no longer Swedish?

As refugees pour into Europe to the tune of thousands every day, politicians like Cecilia forever complain that not enough is being done to help them. Cecilia does talk a lot. She gave "inspiring speeches" at a recent European Jewish Congress in Brussels.** She also led panel discussions at a conference on anti-Semitism where she acted as Vice-Chair of the Working Group on Anti-Semitism.***

Cecilia is knee-deep in just about every bleeding-heart liberal issue one can imagine, and she is, of course, good friends with the proverbial persecuted Jew. What does the Jew say about Cecilia's precious Muslim refugees? Prime Minister of Israel Benjamin Netanyahu said he wants a stronger fence and a bigger wall to keep them out. More precisely he said,

> "We are preparing a multiyear project to encircle Israel with a security fence, to defend ourselves in the Middle East as it is now, and as it is expected to be. They will say to me, what do you want to do, protect the mansion? And the answer is, 'Yes.' What, we will encircle the whole country with a fence and obstacles? The answer is an unequivocal, 'Yes,'" he said. "In the neighborhood in which we live we need to protect ourselves against beasts."****

Beasts. Cecilia, are you inviting beasts to live atop your grandchildren? If so, they will not have the luxury to kvetch all day about the Holocaust like you do.

*https://www.thelocal.se/20150420/children-in-sweden-will-compare-this-to-the-holocaust
**http://www.eurojewcong.org/ejc-in-action/14254-the-ejc-directors-meeting-%E2%80%93-brussels-%E2%80%93-3rd-4th-of-december-2015.html
***http://www.eurojewcong.org/ejc-in-action/14254-the-ejc-directors-meeting-%E2%80%93-brussels-%E2%80%93-3rd-4th-of-december-2015.html
****http://www.independent.co.uk/news/world/middle-east/benjamin-netanyahu-says-he-will-build-a-fence-around-the-whole-of-israel-to-keep-out-the-wild-beasts-a6864841.html

Assimilation?

I saw them every morning. Two women, a mother and daughter, their heads veiled, long pants or long skirts, long sleeves, gloves, even in the heat of a Georgia summer. The weather didn't matter; they remained covered. Every morning I jogged past them with plenty of skin showing. I could feel the sun on my arms. I could feel the wind in my hair. Why shouldn't they? Their heads were down, their eyes scanning the sidewalk immediately in front of them, never looking up, never looking around. Did they even see the flowers? I felt sorry for them.

I saw them every morning. Two women, and I always waved and said hello. They always ignored me, their heads down, their eyes scanning the sidewalk immediately in front of them, never looking up, never looking around. Did they even hear me? They did and they deliberately began to avoid me, turning their heads away, turning their backs to me. Still, every morning, I waved and said hello. It made no difference.

I saw them every morning. Two women, for more than two years. I waved and said hello. I wanted to scream, *look at me!* I wanted to ask them both if they'd ever felt the wind in their hair or the sun on their back. Maybe, in a controlled environment. I felt sorry for them. I wanted to tell them, rip that off and run with me! You don't have to live this way here! But they would have ignored me and moped along, veiled and impervious.

I saw them every morning. Time passed and the pity faded. I began to see them differently, and swallowed a rush of disgust when they passed. How could they see me and other women walk or jog past them, bare arms and legs, hair trailing in the breeze, so happy and free, while they shuffled along, heads down and covered? How could they see that difference and not seem to see anything? Were they happy? They never smiled. They never even looked up.

I saw them every morning, two miserable women walking the same route as if they were lost souls trapped in a repeating cycle. It had been almost three years and I stopped waving. I stopped saying hello. I started wondering why they'd moved here. Maybe they were running from bombs and bullets; I could understand that. What I could never understand is why an immigrant who'd found safe haven would never look up, never say hello, never change or make any attempt to embrace the culture that saved them.

I saw them again not too long ago, walking the same route. It had been a few years since I'd moved to a different neighborhood, but there they were, exactly the same with one significant addition - a baby in a stroller. I laughed when I drove past; maybe that would at long last pull them into the arms of Americana.

May that child be the most stubborn, defiant, rebellious, and American child yet known. May that child wear blue jeans and tank tops, listen to rock and roll, and brazenly celebrate with the loudest of fireworks every Fourth of July. May that child refuse a hijab while eating a hot dog. May that child wave and say hello to the neighbors. May that child be the reason his mother and grandmother finally feel the wind in their hair and the sun on their backs. May that child bring freedom, finally, into their hearts and home.

The Strange Death of Europe

Multi-racial immigration is not working. The immigrants are not assimilating. Europe as a uniquely European continent is disappearing. This is painfully obvious to anyone who does not have his head shoved into the Middle-Eastern sand, and yet our politicians and journalists are tripping over each other to sing the praises of multiculturalism and unfettered immigration. Why? I could speculate myriad possible answers, but the end result is the same - the death of Western civilization.

Look to jolly old England as an example. Whites are a minority in London. There are three million households where not one adult speaks English. From 2001-2011 the number of Muslims rose from 1.5 million to 2.7 million. What happened? Before the 1950s, England was homogeneously white, then came the British Nationality Act and the Commonwealth Immigrants Act, both of which were pushed through Parliament without a word from the British public. They weren't allowed to vote on the matter.

The reason these corrupted politicians gave was labor shortage; the Africans, inter alia, would fill a labor shortage. Well, did they? No. The immigrants had low output, were quarrelsome, irresponsible, ill-disciplined, unintelligent, and volatile; all of this according to an extensive report filed by those who'd attempted to employ them. They were fired as soon as they were hired and that was the end of the failed experiment, and yet immigration continued.
The well-dressed Parliamentarians who caused this continue to claim that mass immigration is good for the economy. Their argument is absolute rubbish. Immigration is a drain on the economy; it cost the Brits alone an estimated 160 billion pounds between 1995 and 2011. What about the population argument? Also rubbish. Most Brits questioned about the matter would have more children if not for the unstable and often violent environment caused by the immigrants, not to mention the higher taxes which are also caused by the immigrants. Hey Parliament! Want more citizens? Encourage your own people to have children instead of importing millions of unassimilable immigrants.

Then there is the diversity argument. Implied in this nonsense is, of course, the idea that Europe was somehow dull and boring. Europe needs new blood to make it interesting! I firmly believe that Europe was plenty interesting before floods of third-world immigrants arrived. Tell me, do you prefer a bed-time story about King Arthur, maybe a Brothers Grimm tale, something from the Norse sagas? Or maybe these dwindling European parents should just issue stern warnings to their children to avoid the no-go zones. Again, rubbish.

Still, the gate openers persist. We have saboteurs like Mona Sahlin, the Swedish Minister of Integration (she's not Swedish) who declares that Swedes are jealous because her people have a rich culture whereas the Swedes only have nonsense like Midsummer Night. What a way to integrate, Mona. Who elected this nay-sayer? Oh, the immigrants who have completely altered the demographic of the country.

Further still, we hear claims that folks like Swedes, Brits, and Germans have no culture. None. As if the Chivalric tales never existed. As if Wagnerian Opera was a mass hallucination. As if the Viking myths were mere whispers on the wind. No culture? Imagine a white man saying that about Africa, India, or Arabia. Heads might explode with the offense it would cause, and yet to say it about Caucasian countries barely warrants the batting of an eye. If this does not make your blood boil, you have been lied to. Find the truth. Keep reading. Keep asking questions. Never bury your head in the sand. Never turn the other cheek unless you are picking up a weapon to defend hearth and home. This is not simple immigration. This is an invasion.

*Statistics are taken from a recent review of the book, *The Strange Death of Europe: Immigration, Identity, Islam* by Douglas Murray, due for release in late June of 2017. The review was written by Andrew Joyce.

American Pie:

Everybody Wants Some

In Balboa Park, San Diego, there are three staring statues of European explorers, standing against the wall in arrogant poise, the one on the left particularly proud, his hand on his hip and a cape thrown casually over his shoulder. He looks as if he's just conquered the world. The trio stares sternly ahead, pleased with themselves and the trail of bodies they've likely left behind.

If they could speak, should they apologize? Does one apologize for being stronger, more advanced, more ambitious? Should they whisper rather than yell, we came, we saw, we…feel so guilty about it? They meant to explore, to claim, to conquer. They meant to convert, even enslave. Why? They saw themselves as Conquistadores, those simply meant to explore and conquer. We may not agree today, but they didn't leave the shores of the Old World today. No, they set sail centuries ago before the modern concept of immigration existed.

When they sailed into the unknown - think of the courage that took - they didn't know what they'd find. Imagine living in ignorance of the geography of roughly half the world. Is it flat, or is it a sphere? It seemed spherical, but the question wasn't quite settled. Here be Monsters? Or there? Go on, *get in the boat anyway*. You may get lost. You may run out of food. You may disappear forever. Go on, *get in the boat anyway*. Could you do it? They did, and they clung to their hopes and dreams as they clung to the hulls of their battered ships, wondering what hell they were sailing into. Still, they were ambitious. They were optimists. They meant to take what they could, if they could, or die trying. Could you do it?

I couldn't, and for that alone I must give these strong souls a begrudging respect. I don't like what happened to the silken haired natives once those boats hit sand, but that changes nothing. Before we judge, we must look at those shores and the wild unknown just beyond the sands through their sun-burned eyes. Step into the body of a fifteenth century Spaniard and look. See what he sees - You've just been on the most harrowing journey of your life. It's been months since you've seen land. Where are you exactly - you have no idea. You're exhausted, probably hungry. There are people here, strange people. Are they friendly? You're not sure. They're not sure. Everyone is…scared. Tensions are high. Anything could happen.

We know what happened, and any number of scenarios could have played out next. Who is to blame? Human nature, ultimately. Those screeching about universal love and acceptance are the same babbling idiots who preach hatred for our shared past. Love, love, love…*but we hate this guy. How dare he succumb to being human!* Where is that hatred for the bloodthirsty Bantu who has ravaged more than half of inner Africa? Where is that hatred for the Choctaw who in a fit of rage after losing his black slaves hunts them down like wild animals? Where is that self-righteous hatred for the marauding bands of rapists who scream to Allah a few times a day, just yesterday? It isn't there. The activist hates only the white man; past, present, and future. Why?

It is a question we must ask ourselves, even if the answer is a thing to go to war about. Before we open the gates to a flood of third-world immigrants because America is a nation of immigrants, we need to understand the nature of those first immigrants. They wouldn't use that word. They wouldn't capitulate. They wouldn't apologize. And so, because of their brazen spirit, we have this country where we are free to moan and groan about old white men, the same white men who ensured our freedom of speech.
Here's another question to ponder: Who has caused this social unrest? The same ilk who would open your country to each and every sorry soul salivating for a piece of American pie. If we continue on this path, there will be no more pie and our hearth will be bare. Everybody wants some? Make your own. Mexican? Make Mexico the place you want to raise your Mexican family. African? Make Africa the fertile breadbasket it should be. Arab? Make the Middle East remember its ancient glory and live it again. American pie isn't for you - you deserve your own, don't you? Go home and make it yourself. *You are capable.* Wait... in marches the Social Justice Warrior, screaming, *but they can't…* What? Those with varying shades of brown skin can't make it without help from magnanimous whites? Wait a minute, you said I was the racist? Maybe not. Paternal racism is still racism.

Once Upon a Dream:

The Emperor's New Dupes Are Knocking at the Gates

MultiCulturalism. It's the mantra of the liberal-minded and like some mind-numbing catechism they mumble it over and over as they silently count their friends of different ethnicities as one might count prayer beads. Like religion, multiCulturalism can be a beautiful thing: it can also poison the mind. For instance, I recently heard someone say, "Oh! Isn't it wonderful!? He's black, gay, half Jewish, and handicapped!" Immediately, I pictured Tiberius standing proudly on the shores of Capri where he kept his collected freaks and I answered, "But what has he *done* to merit your attention? Anything?" Confused silence followed.

This isn't a game and we are not here to collect rare action figures. I don't care one damn bit what color or religion you are. I don't care one damn bit about your sexuality. I don't care if you're in a wheelchair or a war chariot. What matter is this: *What are you doing with your life?* What sort of character do you have? And isn't that the much lauded dream, to judge someone by the content of their character and not a list of superficial bullshit? If so, why am I the bad guy? Why is it racism or bigotry to question one's character or deeds while not giving a god damn about what they look like or what names they give their gods?

There are certain facts that betray a man's character. When waves of so-called refugees sweep into an area and the crime rate skyrockets, this is a statement about their character, not their skin color. It could be argued that their violence is a by-product of their religion, but only one who has studied the religion can argue that and most of those in the multi-cult haven't bothered. What do they do instead? They whine, "What about the good Muslim who lives in my neighborhood? Surely this proves not *all* of them are bad." This needn't be proved as it has never been legitimately questioned. Most are not bad, but then most are not much of anything. The majority is inconsequential, as within every segment of humanity. How many billions of people have lived while mere hundreds adorn the pages of even the most comprehensive world history text? Why? Because not all of them are bad, not all of them are even significant. Most don't matter at all, and so it is and always has been.

But since it keeps coming up, what about those good Muslims? Why aren't they helping refugees in their own countries? Why aren't they speaking out against the abuses of Islam? Where are these moderate Muslims so praised by our liberals? Likely cowering behind their Qurans. They're not allowed to speak out, you see, for fear of dishonor or even death. Still, not all of them are bad, and yet I wonder: How many millions of extremists do we need before we'll be outraged, before we'll speak out against *their* intolerance?

In the name of *our* tolerance, our fear of being labeled a bigot or a racist, we foolishly give our support to those who would destroy our right to offer that tolerance to anyone other than themselves.

They may thank us for the rights we've given them, then auction off our daughters, execute our gay neighbors, crucify the local Christians, and assert their right to multiculturalism, a right to which many will bow down. Of course, not *all* of them will participate. Some will hide in denial. Some will speak out and be persecuted in turn. Some will smile in silent collusion. Countless others will sign up for the latest holy war. But of course, not all of them are bad.

Please, go on, show me percentages. Let's ask the latest victim of gang rape if enough Muslims were involved. Would a mere six or seven be enough if it was your daughter, or do you need *all* of them to rape her before the outrage sets in? Do you see how absurd this argument is? Stop making excuses. Stop collecting humans because you want one in every color on your friends list. Stop pandering for fear of being called racist. It is time to start judging people on the content of their character and countless hordes will NOT pass the test. This is not racism. This is reality.

Demographic Displacement:

The Under-handed Invasion

We've all heard it phrased one way or another - whites and only whites have a moral imperative to become minorities in their own countries. The social justice warriors among us preach tolerance, multiculturalism, and diversity but these are merely feel-good words with negative consequences. One of those consequences is demographic displacement. What that means is that men like Sadiq Khan can become mayor of London and thereby gloss over the needs of his white constituents (you know, the white people who built London up from hut to fort to palace to world power) as he normalizes terrorism and calls any whites who disagree Islamophobic bigots.*

Call me what you will; I'll say it anyway: Muslims do not belong in Europe. Arab peoples belong in Arab countries. White people belong in white countries. But wait, here comes the social justice brigade screaming, "B-b-but America wasn't a white country! You took it!" Well, yes, and we fought tooth and nail for it for a few hundred years before the Declaration of Independence was so brazenly signed, and that happened more than two hundred years ago. Is there a statute of limitations to this nonsense? If not, let's look briefly at Islam.

The Muslims weren't always Muslim. No, Islam spread rapidly at the point of a sword and the imams are still tripping over bodies to get to their prayers on time. Consider Algeria. Enter the wailing and gnashing of teeth anytime memories of French colonialism creep into our thoughts. The French were in Algeria for approximately one hundred years and both Arab and Berber alike are still using their roads, rails, and electricity. When a native Algerian is using any of the modern conveniences left behind by the European, I wonder if he or she remembers that the native population of Algeria wasn't always Arab and it wasn't always Muslim. Oh no, the Muslims have been perched on that pagan, Berber corpse for centuries.

Is that too long ago to file a grievance? With whom do we file a complaint and what is the time limit? A few hundred years? A few thousand? We are wandering into the absurd. Let's say it's a few hundred years. If we use the signing of the Declaration of Independence as a starting point, we Americans need to wait another fifty years plus a few before we can claim this land for whites, once and for all. Ridiculous? Yes it is. Equally ridiculous is pretending that Native Americans were perfectly peaceful, sitting around campfires, stringing turquoise beads, and passing the peace pipe. Some undoubtedly were; thousands more were wearing necklaces made of their neighbors' ears with a scalp or two hanging from blood-stained loin cloths. They were as violent and varied as the rest of us.**

It's time to admit that this country and most lines on present-day maps were staked out in an era when direct and violent conquest was the status quo. If you lost the battle, you lost the land. Over the past few hundred years, however, our most fundamental ideas have changed. Our slaves were emancipated. Universal human rights were decreed and formally recognized. We are expected to respect one another, and so most superficially do.

What is an enemy force to do then if it wants to conquer another's land, take their resources, or destroy its population? It sneaks in destruction through the back door. It deploys violent and disgruntled masses and calls them refugees. It convinces the host population that disagreement is hatred. It displaces and disgraces a culture, piece by piece, until there is nothing left to fight for and it does so in the name of compassion. Those under siege feel powerless even to argue.

This is happening right in front of our eyes. Western civilization is sinking fast. If you are on a lifeboat and the weight is too much, will you throw your own family into the violent sea or will you throw the stranger who is threatening to plunge a knife through the bottom of the boat? The choice must be made before we all drown.

---

*http://www.thegatewaypundit.com/2017/03/outrage-london-mayor-sadiq-khan-says-islamic-terrorism-part-parcel-living-big-city/   This is but one site. A simple Google search yields much more though he is oft misquoted. He actually called for constant vigilance regarding terrorism, which is akin to saying we should expect it. Nonetheless, the troublesome cat is out of the bag.

**Goodrich, Thomas. *Scalp Dance: Indian Warfare on the High Plains*. Stackpole Books, 1997.

Immigration Infection:

The New Colossus and The Undesirables

Walk with me through the creaking metal door at the base of Lady Liberty's pedestal. The air is stale with just a hint of mildew - the rot already palatable. Soon we see it; that beloved poem heard 'round the world, *The New Colossus*:

Not like the brazen giant of Greek fame,

With conquering limbs astride from land to land;

Here at our sea-washed, sunset gates shall stand

A mighty woman with a torch, whose flame

Is the imprisoned lightning, and her name

Mother of Exiles. From her beacon-hand

Glows world-wide welcome; her mild eyes command

The air-bridged harbor that twin cities frame.

"Keep ancient lands your storied pomp!" cries she

With silent lips. "Give me your tired, your poor,

Your huddled masses yearning to breathe free,

The wretched refuse of your teeming shore.

Send these, the homeless, tempest-tossed to me,

I lift my lamp beside the golden door!"

~Emma Lazarus, 1883

If ever there was an eloquent and subtle rending and stabbing of Classical Western civilization, dear reader, you have just read it. Lady Liberty is not like the Colossus of Greek fame; she is, however, quite brazen. This so-called Mother of Exiles, virtue signaling her pathological altruism, is directly calling for the trash of other lands to settle on our shores. While immigration built this country, it was largely the strictly regulated immigration of certain peoples that made America great.

Note the date of the poem, 1883. States rights were slipping away, the ethnicity of our immigrants had begun to shift, and the Federal Reserve was in the midst of one underhanded scheme after another to take over our nation's finances. Fast-forward to 2017 and the results are obvious. The Federal government has become a sort of Greek Hydra and at its heart beats a bank pumping fiat currency through an economy built on the weak backs of the easily exploited. Is this why the Mother of Exiles beckons to the downtrodden? Does she wish to add to the weight of their chains? This is not Liberty.

This new Colossus is not a beacon of freedom but a shrewd manipulator calling the weak to be tied in puppets' strings. She does not want the strong, the brilliant, the proud - these souls are harder to control. Give her instead the tired, poor, and huddled; those ripe for the picking. Are these the immigrants we want? Are these the quality of immigrants who built this country? No.

When the kingdom is already built, however, it is much easier for the rats in the woodpile to get inside the walls and destroy it from the inside out. They've chewed through the ropes on the drawbridge and all matter of vermin can now scurry inside. Our leadership was compromised long ago, and they do not care about the origins of their serfs. Should a segment of these peasants be taller, prouder, stronger than the rest they should be bred out, made to feel ashamed, brainwashed into submission, and, of course, demographically displaced.

This is not what made America great; this will ruin Her. Dear Emma, we do not want anyone's wretched refuse. We do not want huddled masses. We do not want those exiled from every land.

We want the brave, the few, the tall and proud. We want the Old Colossus. We want brazen Greek fame. We want to free the lightning of our old gods, our ancestors, our very souls. We will, in fact, keep the storied pomp of our ancient lands and that spirit can and will live again right here and now.

This New Colossus must be exiled to the depths of the New York harbor. In her place a mighty warrior, that Old Colossus risen again! Yes, he of brazen Western fame, his lightning freed, his storied pomp echoed across the land once more. It is not too late.

Immigration

A Complicated Past, A Complicated Present

Slavery is not just for people of color anymore; in fact, it never was. Rewind to 1771. An ad in the *Virginia Gazette*, dated April 2, reads, "The ship Justitia with about one hundred healthy men, women, and boys…the sale will commence on Tuesday…" Once again, an American Southern colony selling human cargo to work the land. You likely pictured abused Africans, but history is never so black and white. The cargo chained to the hull of this ship was white, and they were sold to the highest bidder – and there are numerous examples. Whatever your high school history teacher told you, the notorious and harrowing "middle passage" was not reserved for the African alone. Not all whites skipped and frolicked onto the decks of luxury liners to come to America for a slice of freedom pie. Countless red necks were nearly broken by shackles on one rat-infested boat after another.

Some came willfully and paid for the privilege. What was their journey like? A German named Middleberger came to America in 1750. He tells us of "smells, fumes, horrors, vomiting…fever, dysentery, headaches, boils, scurvy, mouth-rot, cancer…" He goes on, "In such misery all the people on board pray and cry pitifully together…most of all they cry out against the thieves of human beings."* Yes, thieves. Most of the passengers had been kidnaped, one way or another. It was quite a business – if enough of your cargo survived you'd be a rich man. Alas, many didn't survive. Middleberger tells us of dead women and babies tossed overboard, that there was no food, that he was treated far better than the German cargo chained below deck. Yes, chained. Sadly, his journey was not unusual.
Overall, anywhere from thirty to seventy percent of a given ship's "cargo" died. The survivors were not necessarily the lucky ones. Barbados was a popular destination. What happened there? Most of its "settlers" were prisoners of war thanks to Oliver Cromwell. In fact, it was so common to be forcibly sent there, the term Barbados became a verb. He sent at least one hundred thousand whites off to the new world, in chains. And yes, Cromwell was white too. Meanwhile on the African coast, chiefs black enough to blot out the sun were sending Africans off in chains whenever the price was right. It seems slavery wasn't about one race thinking it was better than another. It was about money and power, but isn't everything?

Back to Barbados, that tropical paradise where eighty percent of whites died in less than twelve months; hence the steady fade to black of slavery, but only after whites became more than eighty-five percent of the slave population in that seventeenth century tourist trap. Now back to jolly ole England, where historians estimate that roughly ten thousand whiteys per year were being kidnaped at home and sold into slavery in the land of the free. This went on for decades in the seventeenth and eighteenth centuries. Four hundred thousand Africans, you cry? Inexcusable. Deplorable. Yes, but if one hundred thousand whites were sent by Cromwell alone to just one island, and ten thousand per year were kidnaped from England alone for decades, and then there were the Germans like the ones chained below deck on Middleberger's typical journey, add to that the lily white Slavs from whom we get the very word slavery as they were so commonly traded like human cattle, and… well, this is getting awkward. Let's just call it a tie. Better yet, let's stop counting. Stop blaming. Stop pointing fingers and pretending that one race is a perpetual victim while the other is solely the villain.

The skewed history we're fed from government textbooks isn't just divisive, it's WRONG. Tell me again, Oh Amistad, how your experience was somehow unique. I hate to burst your overgrown bubble of entitled victimhood, but your suffering was no more nor less than anyone else's on this brutal planet. Thousands upon thousands of whites were kidnaped and sold into slavery while only a fraction of the white population was doing the buying and selling. So, how do we decide who owes who reparations? Do the descendents of the white slaves receive a check or do they sign a check? While we figure that out, let's add to the naughty list those coastal African cousins who, for the right price, sold the South its famous cotton pickers; surely they owe someone something. What about Southern blacks who owned slaves? Yes, they existed. What of folks with mixed heritage – and there's a hell of a lot of them – do they pay themselves? Maybe they should ask Grandma for an extra twenty in their birthday card – just the one Grandma, not the other. Is this getting ridiculous yet? Yes, and it always has been. The very notion of intergenerational guilt is debatable. The sins of the father? No. I don't accept that.

The sins of a few men? Maybe. But who? The past is a blood-soaked disaster and it can't be changed. The present, that's here and now. So what of it? There are right now thousands if not millions of slaves in the Middle East, India, and yes the precious motherland of Africa; to name only three places. What about these poor souls born or sold into chains? No one seems to care. Go on, tell me again about your ancestors forced to work in the heat of the American South. Tell me that AFTER you do something to stop today's slave trade.

Still, it persists, this obsession with the American South. So, let's look at that sweltering spot on the map where I've lived since birth. Here we are fed illusions in school. Here we are taught that only blacks were enslaved. Here we are taught that we are not to trust one another, that one race thinks it's better, that the other race needs special conditions just to get by. Here we are forced to buy into a false perception of lopsided oppression. Here we exist in contrived and illusory conditions that allow only black lives to matter, that perpetuate notions like white privilege. Here we live a lie, until we do just a bit of digging. Scratch the surface of that red Georgia clay and you'll see it – a truth far more complex than your government, left or right, would have you know. We've all been lied to.

True racism isn't found under a starched white hood. It's in the white marble of our nation's capitol; it's in our liberal media; it's in our entertainment; it's ignited in each and every damn one of us whenever we buy into any of their pre-packaged stories from approved reading lists, on screens, in newspapers, in speeches by any one of our laughable candidates. Go on, pick up the race card dealt to you by some political lackey. Play their games. Keep hating each other. Have a riot or two! Give the government a reason to exist. If we governed ourselves, the government would go out of business – and they know it. Some readers may charge me with racism, some with outright hatred. Go ahead. Say what you will, but don't exhaust those standard accusations right away. I'm just getting started.

*Zinn, Howard. *A People's History of the United States*. NY, NY: Harper Perennial, 2015, p.44.

Rainbow Warriors

This is the end, beautiful friend, though the veil will not be lifted. Instead, it's slowly rotting away as our politicians and bankers pull at loose threads. It is the task of the writer, the freethinker, and the revolutionary to weave it anew, even if from the other side. It matters not if you sit at the loom or sharpen your blade. The world needs both pen and sword in this battle.

The masses are rootless, severed from their ancestral source and told we are all one - and this from the same venom-dripping tongues that preach the values of multiculturalism. Multi, that is, unless you are of Norse descent and hold to Asatru. Of African descent? Embrace your voodoo! Of Moorish descent? Let us make concessions for your Islam. Of Celtic descent? Let us scream racist and tear your culture from you the second you start to remember. Teutonic? How dare you bring up anything that stinks of Germanicism.

Why? When ethnic and cultural identity is broken, so is opposition. That is why the puppet masters lead a broken pack into another's land. That is why they preach multiculturalism and oneness, but be warned - this sentimental oneness only comes when the surviving wild ones are bred into the domesticated masses. Will the day come when all wolves lie at the puppet masters' feet? This is the restructuring of society. This is social engineering. This is intentional.

The hypocrisy of the puppeteers is blatant; they've found a way to uproot the discontented masses and given them a common enemy whose past is no more bloodied than anyone else's. This enemy is the one they see as the only remaining foe to be broken - and do they want the white wolf broken, torn to bits, scattered to the multi-colored masses, and forgotten to all but history. Will history remember the white pack fondly? Not likely, as history is the product of the victor and when you write the books you can spill all the blood on one side of the page and the reader who looks no further will see blame only there. The above scenario is not inevitable and history happens every day. There is time enough for the white pack to gather, and that time will come. The time will come when the brown pack comes to resent being led too far from home. The time will come when the black wolf realizes he is being used. That day is nigh, but we are not there yet. There is work to be done.

Today, our roots are severed and the string pullers tell us, "This is your collective past! Look no further!" Look anyway. When you do, you'll see that these storytellers have used a faulty thread and their tales are unraveling. Look again and you'll see the complexities they tried to hide. Look closer still and you'll see blood and tears everywhere.

History is blood. Blood is history. We are all villains. We are all victims. This is the only oneness we should embrace, the oneness of responsibility for an entire species gone horribly awry. If you see right here and wrong there, cut your strings. You're being played. They can play you because you've no roots, nothing to draw strength from, nothing to keep them from jerking you this way and that. Find your roots, talk to your ancestors, embrace your color not as a racist but as one who is racially aware. There is a subtle but crucial difference and that difference is the critical line between exclusivist hatred and an autonomous appreciation of diversity. We can all take pleasure in the beauty of the rainbow and our own unique color within it.

They can play you because you feel powerless; you have forgotten who you are. And on the puppet masters cajole, "Skin color is only superficial; forget about it." Yes, brown is a color painted on the surface, but is Congolese only skin deep? Kenyan? There is a world hiding in those words; find it before it's lost forever. What about yellow? It's just another color, but is Tibetan merely a gloss? No. But surely white is just a color. Of course it is, but is Slavic? Norse? No. When we sever our roots form the spirit behind these colors, we become powerless. Look to the Native American with his coppered skin in all his tattooed and leather-clad glory. Here is a man with strength. Look at him instead in a flannel shirt by a rusted trailer, beer in hand. Here is a man severed, powerless. Did white do that to him? No. The powers that be, colorless souls who only care about gold, did that to him - and to all of us. They aren't finished. Find your roots. Find your power.

Power lies not in mounds of gold, but in the soul of the Viking who remembers the sagas. It lies like a buried treasure in the heart of the Aboriginal who refuses modernity, in the Indian who covers himself with ash and doesn't give a god damn for the rest of the world. Power can be found in the hands of the black Southerner who refuses baptism and instead picks up mask and drum. We are not one. We are many and we are powerful. The hoarders of gold want us to forget that. Whether you remember Christ crucified or Odin nailed to a tree, remember. Remember that both changed their worlds and let the rest of the world have its own stories of greatness. Remember your own stories. Remember that we are not a gray mass but a colorful multitude with the power to cut our strings whether with scimitar, tomahawk, or broadsword. The time has come to choose your blade.

Madness

We are at a proverbial impasse. I can sit here all day and pray to the gods of every nation that the liberal activist sees things my way, but he or she or whatever doesn't believe in the gods, not a single one of them. For such a soul as this, the magic is lost. When the beauty and belief of tradition was ripped from them, those so deeply impoverished in spirit filled the void with fanaticism and their every drop of blood is poisoned, but they don't see it that way.

Even as they condemn the Christian, they cling to their convictions with a fervor that would impress any medieval saint, and yet they can't see the parallels. Their eyes have been gouged out by one too many blockbuster films, their ears run through by one too many professors, their tongues ripped out by a babbling, lying media. And still they adore their torturers. They feel the breaking of their souls as progress, the rending of their spirit as equality, the theft of all they once held dear as justice. Yes, any medieval saint would be impressed if not appalled.

I am appalled. I want them to see the beauty of their bold and unapologetic ancestors. I want them to hear the haunting aura of a Latin Mass, the stirring cadence of a Viking saga, the lilting melody of a hymn to Dionysus. I want them to speak out against the rape of history and the brutal hacking and chopping of their own roots; for the family tree, regardless of origin, dies without roots.

When we march for baseless and raceless equality, we are marching towards the death of the diversity we simultaneously praise. Madness! When we scream for sexual liberation and gender equality, we scream for the death of our race as we demean motherhood and smother the innocence of childhood in its cradle. Madness! When we trash the religions and beliefs of our ancestors even as we rant and rave in protest of anything that hints at anti-semitism or Islamaphobia, we hand our identity and freedoms to a handful of string pullers in the Middle East. Madness!

Those pulling our strings from one side of the globe to another do not think black lives matter. They don't care if you're the house nigger, the field nigger, or the proud African chief. Just fall in line, they say. Have a riot or two. Loot the neighborhood. Rip society to shreds. Mix with the whites. Mix with the Asians. Lose yourself. Forget who you are. When you do, the string pullers will give you a new identity. Tell me, slave, do you like your new name or will you hold onto your African name even under the whip? If black lives do matter, you'll hold onto your roots. You'll remember who you are and where you came from. If black lives matter, the blacks will turn inward and heal their wounds, stop slaughtering each other, stop feeding the prisons. If black lives matter, the blacks will go home and take what is theirs - African soil, African faith, African pride. Go home and tend to your roots. You deserve better than another country's scraps. Those pulling our strings from one side of the globe to another do not care about your gender du jour. They don't care what you identify as. The don't care what bathroom you use or which pronoun you choose, but if they can run small businesses out of town because ma and pa can't afford extra bathrooms or they don't want to bake a gay wedding cake? That they care about – funneling everyone's paltry paychecks into the accounts of a few global corporations while the little guy who can't afford gender-neutral toilets on top of a forced minimum wage hike is hung out to dry. It doesn't matter one damn bit if you're bearded and in a dress, follow the money. You'll see. We have the same enemy…

*Adapted from Rachel Summers' novel, *The Forgetting*. Available now at:
https://www.amazon.com/dp/1976412994/ref=sr_1_2?ie=UTF8&qid=1506083595&sr=8-2&keywords=rachel+summers+forgetting

Historic Words

Pericles' Funeral Oration

The following speech was given by the famed Athenian Pericles after the first battle of the Peloponnesian War as recorded by Thucydides (c.460/455-c.399 BCE) in his Peloponnesian War, Book 2.34-46. Public funerals like this were considered rituals and the speaker chosen was to be a man of great valor and wisdom. Pericles was such a man. His speech is as follows:

"Most of my predecessors in this place have commended him who made this speech part of the law, telling us that it is well that it should be delivered at the burial of those who fall in battle. For myself, I should have thought that the worth which had displayed itself in deeds would be sufficiently rewarded by honours also shown by deeds; such as you now see in this funeral prepared at the people's cost. And I could have wished that the reputations of many brave men were not to be imperilled in the mouth of a single individual, to stand or fall according as he spoke well or ill.

For it is hard to speak properly upon a subject where it is even difficult to convince your hearers that you are speaking the truth.

On the one hand, the friend who is familiar with every fact of the story may think that some point has not been set forth with that fullness which he wishes and knows it to deserve; on the other, he who is a stranger to the matter may be led by envy to suspect exaggeration if he hears anything above his own nature. For men can endure to hear others praised only so long as they can severally persuade themselves of their own ability to equal the actions recounted: when this point is passed, envy comes in and with it incredulity. However, since our ancestors have stamped this custom with their approval, it becomes my duty to obey the law and to try to satisfy your several wishes and opinions as best I may.

"I shall begin with our ancestors: it is both just and proper that they should have the honour of the first mention on an occasion like the present. They dwelt in the country without break in the succession from generation to generation, and handed it down free to the present time by their valour. And if our more remote ancestors deserve praise, much more do our own fathers, who added to their inheritance the empire which we now possess, and spared no pains to be able to leave their acquisitions to us of the present generation. Lastly, there are few parts of our dominions that have not been augmented by those of us here, who are still more or less in the vigour of life; while the mother country has been furnished by us with everything that can enable her to depend on her own resources whether for war or for peace. That part of our history which tells of the military achievements which gave us our several possessions, or of the ready valour with which either we or our fathers stemmed the tide of Hellenic or foreign aggression, is a theme too familiar to my hearers for me to dilate on, and I shall therefore pass it by. But what was the road by which we reached our position, what the form of government under which our greatness grew, what the national habits out of which it sprang; these are questions which I may try to solve before I proceed to my panegyric upon these men; since I think this to be a subject upon which on the present occasion a speaker may properly dwell, and to which the whole assemblage, whether citizens or foreigners, may listen with advantage.

"Our constitution does not copy the laws of neighbouring states; we are rather a pattern to others than imitators ourselves. Its administration favours the many instead of the few; this is why it is called a democracy. If we look to the laws, they afford equal justice to all in their private differences; if no social standing, advancement in public life falls to reputation for capacity, class considerations not being allowed to interfere with merit; nor again does poverty bar the way, if a man is able to serve the state, he is not hindered by the obscurity of his condition. The freedom which we enjoy in our government extends also to our ordinary life. There, far from exercising a jealous surveillance over each other, we do not feel called upon to be angry with our neighbour for doing what he likes, or even to indulge in those injurious looks which cannot fail to be offensive, although they inflict no positive penalty. But all this ease in our private relations does not make us lawless as citizens. Against this fear is our chief safeguard, teaching us to obey the magistrates and the laws, particularly such as regard the protection of the injured, whether they are actually on the statute book, or belong to that code which, although unwritten, yet cannot be broken without acknowledged disgrace.

"Further, we provide plenty of means for the mind to refresh itself from business. We celebrate games and sacrifices all the year round, and the elegance of our private establishments forms a daily source of pleasure and helps to banish the spleen; while the magnitude of our city draws the produce of the world into our harbour, so that to the Athenian the fruits of other countries are as familiar a luxury as those of his own.

"If we turn to our military policy, there also we differ from our antagonists. We throw open our city to the world, and never by alien acts exclude foreigners from any opportunity of learning or observing, although the eyes of an enemy may occasionally profit by our liberality; trusting less in system and policy than to the native spirit of our citizens; while in education, where our rivals from their very cradles by a painful discipline seek after manliness, at Athens we live exactly as we please, and yet are just as ready to encounter every legitimate danger. In proof of this it may be noticed that the Lacedaemonians do not invade our country alone, but bring with them all their confederates; while we Athenians advance unsupported into the territory of a neighbour, and fighting upon a foreign soil usually vanquish with ease men who are defending their homes. Our united force was never yet encountered by any enemy, because we have at once to attend to our marine and to dispatch our citizens by land upon a hundred different services; so that, wherever they engage with some such fraction of our strength, a success against a detachment is magnified into a victory over the nation, and a defeat into a reverse suffered at the hands of our entire people. And yet if with habits not of labour but of ease, and courage not of art but of nature, we are still willing to encounter danger, we have the double advantage of escaping the experience of hardships in anticipation and of facing them in the hour of need as fearlessly as those who are never free from them.

"Nor are these the only points in which our city is worthy of admiration. We cultivate refinement without extravagance and knowledge without effeminacy; wealth we employ more for use than for show, and place the real disgrace of poverty not in owning to the fact but in declining the struggle against it. Our public men have, besides politics, their private affairs to attend to, and our ordinary citizens, though occupied with the pursuits of industry, are still fair judges of public matters; for, unlike any other nation, regarding him who takes no part in these duties not as unambitious but as useless, we Athenians are able to judge at all events if we cannot originate, and, instead of looking on discussion as a stumbling-block in the way of action, we think it an indispensable preliminary to any wise action at all. Again, in our enterprises we present the singular spectacle of daring and deliberation, each carried to its highest point, and both united in the same persons; although usually decision is the fruit of ignorance, hesitation of reflection. But the palm of courage will surely be adjudged most justly to those, who best know the difference between hardship and pleasure and yet are never tempted to shrink from danger. In generosity we are equally singular, acquiring our friends by conferring, not by receiving, favours. Yet, of course, the doer of the favour is the firmer friend of the two, in order by continued kindness to keep the recipient in his debt; while the debtor feels less keenly from the very consciousness that the return he makes will be a payment, not a free gift. And it is only the Athenians, who, fearless of consequences, confer their benefits not from calculations of expediency, but in the confidence of liberality.

"In short, I say that as a city we are the school of Hellas, while I doubt if the world can produce a man who, where he has only himself to depend upon, is equal to so many emergencies, and graced by so happy a versatility, as the Athenian. And that this is no mere boast thrown out for the occasion, but plain matter of fact, the power of the state acquired by these habits proves. For Athens alone of her contemporaries is found when tested to be greater than her reputation, and alone gives no occasion to her assailants to blush at the antagonist by whom they have been worsted, or to her subjects to question her title by merit to rule. Rather, the admiration of the present and succeeding ages will be ours, since we have not left our power without witness, but have shown it by mighty proofs; and far from needing a Homer for our panegyrist, or other of his craft whose verses might charm for the moment only for the impression which they gave to melt at the touch of fact, we have forced every sea and land to be the highway of our daring, and everywhere, whether for evil or for good, have left imperishable monuments behind us. Such is the Athens for which these men, in the assertion of their resolve not to lose her, nobly fought and died; and well may every one of their survivors be ready to suffer in her cause.

"Indeed if I have dwelt at some length upon the character of our country, it has been to show that our stake in the struggle is not the same as theirs who have no such blessings to lose, and also that the panegyric of the men over whom I am now speaking might be by definite proofs established. That panegyric is now in a great measure complete; for the Athens that I have celebrated is only what the heroism of these and their like have made her, men whose fame, unlike that of most Hellenes, will be found to be only commensurate with their deserts. And if a test of worth be wanted, it is to be found in their closing scene, and this not only in cases in which it set the final seal upon their merit, but also in those in which it gave the first intimation of their having any. For there is justice in the claim that steadfastness in his country's battles should be as a cloak to cover a man's other imperfections; since the good action has blotted out the bad, and his merit as a citizen more than outweighed his demerits as an individual. But none of these allowed either wealth with its prospect of future enjoyment to unnerve his spirit, or poverty with its hope of a day of freedom and riches to tempt him to shrink from danger. No, holding that vengeance upon their enemies was more to be desired than any personal blessings, and reckoning this to be the most glorious of hazards, they joyfully determined to accept the risk, to make sure of their vengeance, and to let their wishes wait; and while committing to hope the uncertainty of final success, in the business before them they thought fit to act boldly and trust in themselves. Thus choosing to die resisting, rather than to live submitting, they fled only from dishonour, but met danger face to face, and after one brief moment, while at the summit of their fortune, escaped, not from their fear, but from their glory.

"So died these men as became Athenians. You, their survivors, must determine to have as unfaltering a resolution in the field, though you may pray that it may have a happier issue. And not contented with ideas derived only from words of the advantages which are bound up with the defence of your country, though these would furnish a valuable text to a speaker even before an audience so alive to them as the present, you must yourselves realize the power of Athens, and feed your eyes upon her from day to day, till love of her fills your hearts; and then, when all her greatness shall break upon you, you must reflect that it was by courage, sense of duty, and a keen feeling of honour in action that men were enabled to win all this, and that no personal failure in an enterprise could make them consent to deprive their country of their valour, but they laid it at her feet as the most glorious contribution that they could offer. For this offering of their lives made in common by them all they each of them individually received that renown which never grows old, and for a sepulchre, not so much that in which their bones have been deposited, but that noblest of shrines wherein their glory is laid up to be eternally remembered upon every occasion on which deed or story shall call for its commemoration. For heroes have the whole earth for their tomb; and in lands far from their own, where the column with its epitaph declares it, there is enshrined in every breast a record unwritten with no tablet to preserve it, except that of the heart. These take as your model and, judging happiness to be the fruit of freedom and freedom of valour, never decline the dangers of war. For it is not the miserable that would most justly be unsparing of their lives; these have nothing to hope for: it is rather they to whom continued life may bring reverses as yet unknown, and to whom a fall, if it came, would be most tremendous in its consequences. And surely, to a man of spirit, the degradation of cowardice must be immeasurably more grievous than the unfelt death which strikes him in the midst of his strength and patriotism!

"Comfort, therefore, not condolence, is what I have to offer to the parents of the dead who may be here. Numberless are the chances to which, as they know, the life of man is subject; but fortunate indeed are they who draw for their lot a death so glorious as that which has caused your mourning, and to whom life has been so exactly measured as to terminate in the happiness in which it has been passed. Still I know that this is a hard saying, especially when those are in question of whom you will constantly be reminded by seeing in the homes of others blessings of which once you also boasted: for grief is felt not so much for the want of what we have never known, as for the loss of that to which we have been long accustomed. Yet you who are still of an age to beget children must bear up in the hope of having others in their stead; not only will they help you to forget those whom you have lost, but will be to the state at once a reinforcement and a security; for never can a fair or just policy be expected of the citizen who does not, like his fellows, bring to the decision the interests and apprehensions of a father. While those of you who have passed your prime must congratulate yourselves with the thought that the best part of your life was fortunate, and that the brief span that remains will be cheered by the fame of the departed. For it is only the love of honour that never grows old; and honour it is, not gain, as some would have it, that rejoices the heart of age and helplessness.

"Turning to the sons or brothers of the dead, I see an arduous struggle before you. When a man is gone, all are wont to praise him, and should your merit be ever so transcendent, you will still find it difficult not merely to overtake, but even to approach their renown. The living have envy to contend with, while those who are no longer in our path are honoured with a goodwill into which rivalry does not enter. On the other hand, if I must say anything on the subject of female excellence to those of you who will now be in widowhood, it will be all comprised in this brief exhortation. Great will be your glory in not falling short of your natural character; and greatest will be hers who is least talked of among the men, whether for good or for bad.

"My task is now finished. I have performed it to the best of my ability, and in word, at least, the requirements of the law are now satisfied. If deeds be in question, those who are here interred have received part of their honours already, and for the rest, their children will be brought up till manhood at the public expense: the state thus offers a valuable prize, as the garland of victory in this race of valour, for the reward both of those who have fallen and their survivors. And where the rewards for merit are greatest, there are found the best citizens.
"And now that you have brought to a close your lamentations for your relatives, you may depart."

https://online.hillsdale.edu/document.doc?id=355
https://sourcebooks.fordham.edu/ancient/pericles-funeralspeech.asp

The Declaration of Independence

When, in the course of human events, it becomes necessary for one people to dissolve the political bonds which have connected them with another, and to assume among the powers of the earth, the separate and equal station to which the laws of nature and of nature's God entitle them, a decent respect to the opinions of mankind requires that they should declare the causes which impel them to the separation.

We hold these truths to be self-evident, that all men are created equal, that they are endowed by their Creator with certain unalienable rights, that among these are life, liberty and the pursuit of happiness. That to secure these rights, governments are instituted among men, deriving their just powers from the consent of the governed. That whenever any form of government becomes destructive to these ends, it is the right of the people to alter or to abolish it, and to institute new government, laying its foundation on such principles and organizing its powers in such form, as to them shall seem most likely to effect their safety and happiness. Prudence, indeed, will dictate that governments long established should not be changed for light and transient causes; and accordingly all experience hath shown that mankind are more disposed to suffer, while evils are sufferable, than to right themselves by abolishing the forms to which they are accustomed. But when a long train of abuses and usurpations, pursuing invariably the same object evinces a design to reduce them under absolute despotism, it is their right, it is their duty, to throw off such government, and to provide new guards for their future security. —

Such has been the patient sufferance of these colonies; and such is now the necessity which constrains them to alter their former systems of government. The history of the present King of Great Britain is a history of repeated injuries and usurpations, all having in direct object the establishment of an absolute tyranny over these states. To prove this, let facts be submitted to a candid world.

He has refused his assent to laws, the most wholesome and necessary for the public good.

He has forbidden his governors to pass laws of immediate and pressing importance, unless suspended in their operation till his assent should be obtained; and when so suspended, he has utterly neglected to attend to them.

He has refused to pass other laws for the accommodation of large districts of people, unless those people would relinquish the right of representation in the legislature, a right inestimable to them and formidable to tyrants only.

He has called together legislative bodies at places unusual, uncomfortable, and distant from the depository of their public records, for the sole purpose of fatiguing them into compliance with his measures.

He has dissolved representative houses repeatedly, for opposing with manly firmness his invasions on the rights of the people.

He has refused for a long time, after such dissolutions, to cause others to be elected; whereby the legislative powers, incapable of annihilation, have returned to the people at large for their exercise; the state remaining in the meantime exposed to all the dangers of invasion from without, and convulsions within.

He has endeavored to prevent the population of these states; for that purpose obstructing the laws for naturalization of foreigners; refusing to pass others to encourage their migration hither, and raising the conditions of new appropriations of lands.

He has obstructed the administration of justice, by refusing his assent to laws for establishing judiciary powers.

He has made judges dependent on his will alone, for the tenure of their offices, and the amount and payment of their salaries.

He has erected a multitude of new offices, and sent hither swarms of officers to harass our people, and eat out their substance.
He has kept among us, in times of peace, standing armies without the consent of our legislature.

He has affected to render the military independent of and superior to civil power.

He has combined with others to subject us to a jurisdiction foreign to our constitution, and unacknowledged by our laws; giving his assent to their acts of pretended legislation:

For quartering large bodies of armed troops among us:
For protecting them, by mock trial, from punishment for any murders which they should commit on the inhabitants of these states:
For cutting off our trade with all parts of the world:
For imposing taxes on us without our consent:
For depriving us in many cases, of the benefits of trial by jury:
For transporting us beyond seas to be tried for pretended offenses:
For abolishing the free system of English laws in a neighboring province, establishing therein an arbitrary government, and enlarging its boundaries so as to render it at once an example and fit instrument for introducing the same absolute rule in these colonies:
For taking away our charters, abolishing our most valuable laws, and altering fundamentally the forms of our governments:
For suspending our own legislatures, and declaring themselves invested with power to legislate for us in all cases whatsoever.
He has abdicated government here, by declaring us out of his protection and waging war against us.

He has plundered our seas, ravaged our coasts, burned our towns, and destroyed the lives of our people.

He is at this time transporting large armies of foreign mercenaries to complete the works of death, desolation and tyranny, already begun with circumstances of cruelty and perfidy scarcely paralleled in the most barbarous ages, and totally unworthy the head of a civilized nation.

He has constrained our fellow citizens taken captive on the high seas to bear arms against their country, to become the executioners of their friends and brethren, or to fall themselves by their hands.

He has excited domestic insurrections amongst us, and has endeavored to bring on the inhabitants of our frontiers, the merciless Indian savages, whose known rule of warfare, is undistinguished destruction of all ages, sexes and conditions.
In Jefferson's draft there is a part on slavery here

In every stage of these oppressions we have petitioned for redress in the most humble terms: our repeated petitions have been answered only by repeated injury. A prince, whose character is thus marked by every act which may define a tyrant, is unfit to be the ruler of a free people.

Nor have we been wanting in attention to our British brethren. We have warned them from time to time of attempts by their legislature to extend an unwarrantable jurisdiction over us. We have reminded them of the circumstances of our emigration and settlement here. We have appealed to their native justice and magnanimity, and we have conjured them by the ties of our common kindred to disavow these usurpations, which, would inevitably interrupt our connections and correspondence. We must, therefore, acquiesce in the necessity, which denounces our separation, and hold them, as we hold the rest of mankind, enemies in war, in peace friends.

We, therefore, the representatives of the United States of America, in General Congress, assembled, appealing to the Supreme Judge of the world for the rectitude of our intentions, do, in the name, and by the authority of the good people of these colonies, solemnly publish and declare, that these united colonies are, and of right ought to be free and independent states; that they are absolved from all allegiance to the British Crown, and that all political connection between them and the state of Great Britain, is and ought to be totally dissolved; and that as free and independent states, they have full power to levy war, conclude peace, contract alliances, establish commerce, and to do all other acts and things which independent states may of right do. And for the support of this declaration, with a firm reliance on the protection of Divine Providence, we mutually pledge to each other our lives, our fortunes and our sacred honor.

JOHN HANCOCK, President

Attested, CHARLES THOMSON, Secretary

New Hampshire – JOSIAH BARTLETT WILLIAM WHIPPLE MATTHEW THORNTON
Massachusetts-Bay – SAMUEL ADAMS JOHN ADAMS ROBERT TREAT PAINE
ELBRIDGE GERRY
Rhode Island – STEPHEN HOPKINS WILLIAM ELLERY
Connecticut – ROGER SHERMAN SAMUEL HUNTINGTON WILLIAM WILLIAMS
OLIVER WOLCOTT
Georgia – BUTTON GWINNETT LYMAN HALL GEO. WALTON
Maryland – SAMUEL CHASE WILLIAM PACA THOMAS STONE CHARLES CARROLL
Virginia – GEORGE WYTHE RICHARD HENRY LEE THOMAS JEFFERSON BENJAMIN
HARRISON THOMAS NELSON, JR. FRANCIS LIGHTFOOT LEE CARTER BRAXTON.

New York – WILLIAM FLOYD PHILIP LIVINGSTON FRANCIS LEWIS LEWIS MORRIS
Pennsylvania – ROBERT MORRIS BENJAMIN RUSH BENJAMIN FRANKLIN
JOHN MORTON GEORGE CLYMER JAMES SMITH GEORGE TAYLOR
JAMES WILSON GEORGE ROSS
Delaware – CAESAR RODNEY GEORGE READ THOMAS M'KEAN
North Carolina – WILLIAM HOOPER JOSEPH HEWES JOHN PENN
South Carolina – EDWARD RUTLEDGE THOMAS HEYWARD, JR. THOMAS LYNCH, JR.
ARTHUR MIDDLETON
New Jersey – RICHARD STOCKTON JOHN WITHERSPOON FRANCIS HOPKINS
JOHN HART ABRAHAM CLARK

http://www.ushistory.org/declaration/document/

Deus Volt

It was a blustery autumn day in the year of our lord, 1095, when Pope Urban II called all of Christendom to a Crusade against Muslim encroachment in the East. His call was answered and *Deus Volt* rang loud and clear across each and every Catholic kingdom in Western Europe and beyond. The call may be heard again, and soon, but today's useless Pope will not be the source of this battle cry. Frustrated citizens from the northern-most reaches of Sweden to the overrun Italian isles may well scream it for all the world to hear. Listen. Whether Catholic, Protestant, Heathen, or Heretic - Listen and heed the call.

Pope Urban's Speech:

"We have heard the message of the Christians of the East. It described to you the lamentable situation of Jerusalem and the people of God. It described how the city of the King of Kings, which transmitted the pure Faith to all the other cities, was obliged to pay service to pagan superstitions. And how the miraculous Sepulcher where death could not guard its Prisoner, the Sepulcher which is the source of future life and, above all, where the Sun of the Resurrection rose, was befouled by those who will not rise again except to serve as straw for the eternal fire.

"A victorious impiety has suffused the most fertile lands of Asia in darkness. The cities of Antioch, Ephesus and Nicaea already are taken by the Musselmen. The barbarous hordes of Turks pitch their standards at the very borders of Hellespoint [where the Aegean Sea meets the Sea of Marmara], where they threaten all the Christian nations. If the one true God does not contain their triumphant march, arming their children, what nation, what kingdom will be able to close the doors of the West to them? "The people worthy of glory, the people blessed by God Our Lord, moan and fall under the weight of these outrages and most shameful humiliations. The race of the elect suffers outrageous persecutions, and the impious race of the Saracens respects neither the virgins of the Lord nor the colleges of priests. They run over the weak and the elderly, they seize the children from their mothers so that they might forget, among the barbarians, the name of God. That perverse nation profanes the hospices … The temple of the Lord is treated like a criminal and the ornaments of the sanctuary are robbed. "What more shall I say to you? "We are disgraced, sons and brothers, who live in these days of calamities! Can we look at the world in this century reproved by Heaven to witness the desolation of the Holy City and remain in peace while it is so oppressed? Is it not preferable to die in war rather than suffer any longer so horrible a spectacle? Let us all weep for our faults that raise the divine ire, yes, let us weep… But let not our tears be like the seed thrown into the sand. Let the fire of our repentance raise up the Holy War and the love of our brethren lead us into combat. Let our lives be stronger than death to fight against the enemies of the Christian people."

DO NOT COWARDLY STAY IN YOUR HOMES.

The Pontiff continued: "Warriors who hear my voice, you who will go to war, rejoice, because you are taking up a legitimate war … Arm yourselves with the sword of the Maccabees and go to defend the house of Israel who is the daughter of the Lord of Armies.

"It is no longer a matter of avenging just the injuries made to men, but rather those made to God. It is no longer a matter of attacking a city or a castle, but of conquering the Holy Places. If you triumph, the blessings of Heaven and the kingdoms of Asia will be your reward. If you succumb, you will achieve the glory of dying in the same Land where Jesus Christ died, and God will not forget that He saw you in the Holy Militia. "Do not cowardly stay in your homes with profane affections and sentiments. Soldiers of God, hear nothing but the laments of Sion. Break all your earthly bonds and remember what the Lord said: "He who loves father or mother more than Me is not worthy of Me…. And every one that forsakes his houses, or brethren, or sisters, or father, or mother, or wife, or children, or lands, for My name's sake, shall receive a hundredfold, and shall inherit everlasting life." This speech of Urban II touched the hearts of all. It seemed as if an ardent flame had descended from Heaven. The assembly, taken by an enthusiasm that no mere human eloquence had inspired, raised up in a mass and shouted: "Deus vult! Deus vult!" [God desires it! God desires it!"] When silence was reestablished, the Holy Pontiff continued: "Behold here today is fulfilled in you the promise of the Lord who said that where His disciples are gathered together in His name, He is there in the midst of them. If the Savior of the world is now among you, it was He who inspired that which I have just heard. It was He who has drawn forth from you this war-cry, 'God desires it!' and let it be raised everywhere as witness to the presence of the Lord God of Armies!" The Pope raised up before the assembly the Cross, the sign of Redemption, and said: "It is Jesus Christ Himself who leaves His Sepulcher and presents to you His Cross. It will be the sign that will unite the dispersed children of Israel. Raise it to your shoulders and place it on your chests. Let it shine on your arms and banners. Let it be for you the reward of victory or the palm of martyrdom. It will be an unceasing reminder that Our Lord died for us and we should die for Him."

Miracles

"Receive this sword in the Name of the Father, and of the Son, and of the Holy Ghost." The priest of each parish blessed the arms that were piled up before him. He begged the All-Powerful Lord to grant to those who would bear them the valor and strength that led David to defeat the unfaithful Goliath. Upon delivering to each knight the sword that had been blessed, the priest would say: "Receive this sword in the Name of the Father, and of the Son, and of the Holy Ghost. May it serve you for the triumph of the Faith. However, do not shed innocent blood with it." After sprinkling the standards of the Cross with holy water, he delivered them over, saying, "Go to combat for the glory of God and let this sign make you triumph in all dangers."

A Den of Vipers

Andrew Jackson ~ Speech to Congress on July 10, 1832

A BANK of the United States is in many respects convenient for the Government and useful to the people. Entertaining this opinion, and deeply impressed with the belief that some of the powers and privileges possessed by the existing Bank are unauthorized by the Constitution, subversive of the rights of the States, and dangerous to the liberties of the people, I felt it my duty, at an early period of my administration, to call the attention of Congress to the practicability of organizing an institution combining all its advantages, and obviating these objections. I sincerely regret that, in the act before me, I can perceive none of those modifications of the Bank charter which are necessary, in my opinion, to make it compatible with justice, with sound policy, or with the Constitution of our country.

Every monopoly, and all exclusive privileges, are granted at the expense of the public, which ought to receive a fair equivalent. The many millions which this act proposes to bestow on the stockholders of the existing Bank must come directly or indirectly out of the earnings of the American people. It is due to them, therefore, if their Government sell monopolies and exclusive privileges, that they should at least exact for them as much as they are worth in open market. The value of the monopoly in this case may be correctly ascertained. The twenty-eight millions of stock would probably be at an advance of fifty per cent, and command in market at least forty-two millions of dollars, subject to the payment of the present bonus. The present value of the monopoly, therefore, is seventeen millions of dollars, and this the act proposes to sell for three millions, payable in fifteen annual installments of two hundred thousand dollars each.

It is not conceivable how the present stockholders can have any claim to the special favor of the Government. The present corporation has enjoyed its monopoly during the period stipulated in the original contract. If we must have such a corporation, why should not the Government sell out the whole stock, and thus secure to the people the full market value of the privileges granted? Why should not Congress create and sell twenty-eight millions of stock, incorporating the purchasers with all the powers and privileges secured in this act, and putting the premium upon the sales into the Treasury.

It has been urged as an argument in favor of rechartering the present Bank, that the calling in its loans will produce great embarrassment and distress. The time allowed to close its concerns is ample; and if it has been well managed, its pressure will be light, and heavy only in case its management has been bad. If, therefore, it shall produce distress, the fault will be its own: and it would furnish a reason against renewing a power which has been so obviously abused. But will there ever be a time when this reason will be less powerful? To acknowledge its force is to admit that the Bank ought to be perpetual; and, as a consequence, the present stockholders, and those inheriting their rights as successors, be established a privileged order, clothed both with great political power and enjoying immense pecuniary advantages from their connection with the Government. The modifications of the existing charter, proposed by this act, are not such, in my views, as make it consistent with the rights of the States or the liberties of the people.

Is there no danger to our liberty and independence in a Bank that in its nature has so little to bind it to our country. The president of the Bank has told us that most of the State banks exist by its forbearance. Should its influence become concentered, as it may under the operation of such an act as this, in the hands of a self-elected directory, whose interests are identified with those of the foreign stockholders, will there not be cause to tremble for the purity of our elections in peace, and for the independence of our country in war. Their power would be great whenever they might choose to exert it; but if this monopoly were regularly renewed every fifteen or twenty years, on terms proposed by themselves, they might seldom in peace put forth their strength to influence elections or control the affairs of the nation. But if any private citizen or public functionary should interpose to curtail its powers, or prevent a renewal of its privileges, it cannot be doubted that he would be made to feel its influence.

Should the stock of the Bank principally pass into the hands of the subjects of a foreign country, and we should unfortunately become involved in a war with that country, what would be our condition? Of the course which would be pursued by a bank almost wholly owned by the subjects of a foreign power, and managed by those whose interests, if not affections, would run in the same direction, there can be no doubt. All its operations within would be in aid of the hostile fleets and armies without. Controlling our currency, receiving our public moneys, and holding thousands of our citizens in dependence, it would be more formidable and dangerous than the naval and military power of the enemy....

It is maintained by the advocates of the Bank, that its constitutionality, in all its features, ought to be considered as settled by precedent, and by the decision of the Supreme Court. To this conclusion I cannot assent. Mere precedent is a dangerous source of authority, and should not be regarded as deciding questions of constitutional power, except where the acquiescence of the people and the States can be considered as well settled. So far from this being the case on this subject, an argument against the Bank might be based on precedent. One Congress, in 1791, decided in favor of a bank; another, in 1811, decided against it. One Congress, in 1815, decided against a bank; another, in 1816, decided in its favor. Prior to the present Congress, therefore, the precedents drawn from that source were equal. If we resort to the States, the expressions of legislative, judicial, and executive opinions against the Bank have been probably to those in its favor as four to one. There is nothing in precedent, therefore, which, if its authority were admitted, ought to weigh in favor of the act before me.

If the opinion of the Supreme Court covered the whole ground of this act, it ought not to control the coordinate authorities of this Government. The Congress, the Executive, and the Court, must each for itself be guided by its own opinion of the Constitution. Each public officer, who takes an oath to support the Constitution, swears that he will support it as he understands it, and not as it is understood by others. It is as much the duty of the House of Representatives, of the Senate, and of the President to decide upon the constitutionality of any bill or resolution which may be presented to them for passage or approval as it is of the supreme judges when it may be brought before them for judicial decision....

It cannot be necessary to the character of the Bank as a fiscal agent of the Government that its private business should be exempted from that taxation to which all the State banks are liable; nor can I conceive it proper that the substantive and most essential powers reserved by the States shall be thus attacked and annihilated as a means of executing the powers delegated to the general government. It may be safely assumed that none of those sages who had an agency in forming or adopting our Constitution, ever imagined that any portion of the taxing power of the States, not prohibited to them nor delegated to Congress, was to be swept away and annihilated as a means of executing certain powers delegated to Congress…

Suspicions are entertained, and charges are made, of gross abuse and violation of its charter. An investigation unwillingly conceded, and so restricted in time as necessarily to make it incomplete and unsatisfactory, disclosed enough to excite suspicion and alarm. In the practices of the principal bank partially unveiled, in the absence of important witnesses, and in numerous charges confidently made, and as yet wholly uninvestigated, there was enough to induce a majority of the committee of investigation, a committee which was selected from the most able and honorable members of the House of Representatives, to recommend a suspension of further action upon the bill, and a prosecution of the inquiry. As the charter had yet four years to run, and as a renewal now was not necessary to the successful prosecution of its business, it was to have been expected that the Bank itself, conscious of its purity, and proud of its character, would have withdrawn its application for the present, and demanded the severest scrutiny into all its transactions. In their declining to do so, there seems to be an additional reason why the functionaries of the Government should proceed with less haste and more caution in the renewal of their monopoly….

I have now done my duty to my country. If sustained by my fellow citizens, I shall be grateful and happy; if not, I shall find in the motives which impel me ample grounds for contentment and peace. In the difficulties which surround us and the dangers which threaten our institutions there is cause for neither dismay nor alarm. For relief and deliverance let us firmly rely on that kind Providence which, I am sure, watches with peculiar care over the destinies of our republic, and on the intelligence and wisdom of our countrymen. Through His abundant goodness, and their patriotic devotion, our liberty and Union will be preserved.

Congressman McFadden on the Federal Reserve
June 10, 1932

The Federal Reserve – A Corrupt Institution

"Mr. Chairman, we have in this Country one of the most corrupt institutions the world has ever known. I refer to the Federal Reserve Board and the Federal Reserve Banks, hereinafter called the Fed. The Fed has cheated the Government of these United States and the people of the United States out of enough money to pay the Nation's debt. The depredations and iniquities of the Fed has cost enough money to pay the National debt several times over.

"This evil institution has impoverished and ruined the people of these United States, has bankrupted itself, and has practically bankrupted our Government. It has done this through the defects of the law under which it operates, through the maladministration of that law by the Fed and through the corrupt practices of the moneyed vultures who control it.

"Some people who think that the Federal Reserve Banks United States Government institutions. They are private monopolies which prey upon the people of these United States for the benefit of themselves and their foreign customers; foreign and domestic speculators and swindlers; and rich and predatory money lender. In that dark crew of financial pirates there are those who would cut a man's throat to get a dollar out of his pocket; there are those who send money into states to buy votes to control our legislatures; there are those who maintain International propaganda for the purpose of deceiving us into granting of new concessions which will permit them to cover up their past misdeeds and set again in motion their gigantic train of crime.

"These twelve private credit monopolies were deceitfully and disloyally foisted upon this Country by the bankers who came here from Europe and repaid us our hospitality by undermining our American institutions. Those bankers took money out of this Country to finance Japan in a war against Russia. They created a reign of terror in Russia with our money in order to help that war along. They instigated the separate peace between Germany and Russia, and thus drove a wedge between the allies in World War. They financed Trotsky's passage from New York to Russia so that he might assist in the destruction of the Russian Empire. They fomented and instigated the Russian Revolution, and placed a large fund of American dollars at Trotsky's disposal in one of their branch banks in Sweden so that through him Russian homes might be thoroughly broken up and Russian children flung far and wide from their natural protectors. They have since begun breaking up of American homes and the dispersal of American children. "Mr. Chairman, there should be no partisanship in matters concerning banking and currency affairs in this Country, and I do not speak with any.

"In 1912 the National Monetary Association, under the chairmanship of the late Senator Nelson W. Aldrich, made a report and presented a vicious bill called the National Reserve Association bill. This bill is usually spoken of as the Aldrich bill. Senator Aldrich did not write the Aldrich bill. He was the tool, if not the accomplice, of the European bankers who for nearly twenty years had been scheming to set up a central bank in this Country and who in 1912 has spent and were continuing to spend vast sums of money to accomplish their purpose.

"We were opposed to the Aldrich plan for a central bank. The men who rule the Democratic Party then promised the people that if they were returned to power there would be no central bank established here while they held the reigns of government. Thirteen months later that promise was broken, and the Wilson administration, under the tutelage of those sinister Wall Street figures who stood behind Colonel House, established here in our free Country the worm-eaten monarchical institution of the "King's Bank" to control us from the top downward, and from the cradle to the grave.

"The Federal Reserve Bank destroyed our old and characteristic way of doing business. It discriminated against our 1-name commercial paper, the finest in the world, and it set up the antiquated 2-name paper, which is the present curse of this Country and which wrecked every country which has ever given it scope; it fastened down upon the Country the very tyranny from which the framers of the Constitution sough to save us.

PRESIDENT JACKSON'S TIME

"One of the greatest battles for the preservation of this Republic was fought out here in Jackson's time; when the second Bank of the United States, founded on the same false principles of those which are here exemplified in the Fed was hurled out of existence. After that, in 1837, the Country was warned against the dangers that might ensue if the predatory interests after being cast out should come back in disguise and unite themselves to the Executive and through him acquire control of the Government. That is what the predatory interests did when they came back in the livery of hypocrisy and under false pretenses obtained the passage of the Fed.

"The danger that the Country was warned against came upon us and is shown in the long train of horrors attendant upon the affairs of the traitorous and dishonest Fed. Look around you when you leave this Chamber and you will see evidences of it in all sides. This is an era of misery and for the conditions that caused that misery, the Fed are fully liable. This is an era of financed crime and in the financing of crime the Fed does not play the part of a disinterested spectator.

"It has been said that the draughts man who was employed to write the text of the Aldrich bill because that had been drawn up by lawyers, by acceptance bankers of European origin in New York. It was a copy, in general a translation of the statues of the Reichsbank and other European central banks. One-half million dollars was spent on the part of the propaganda organized by these bankers for the purpose of misleading public opinion and giving Congress the impression that there was an overwhelming popular demand for it and the kind of currency that goes with it, namely, an asset currency based on human debts and obligations. Dr. H. Parker Willis had been employed by Wall Street and propagandists, and when the Aldrich measure failed- he obtained employment with Carter Glass, to assist in drawing the banking bill for the Wilson administration. He appropriated the text of the Aldrich bill. There is no secret about it. The test of the Federal Reserve Act was tainted from the first.

"A few days before the bill came to a vote, Senator Henry Cabot Lodge, of Massachusetts, wrote to Senator John W. Weeks as follows:

New York City,
December 17, 1913

"'My Dear Senator Weeks:

"'Throughout my public life I have supported all measures designed to take the Government out of the banking business. This bill puts the Government into the banking business as never before in our history. "'The powers vested in the Federal Reserve Board seen to me highly dangerous especially where there is political control of the Board. I should be sorry to hold stock in a bank subject to such dominations. The bill as it stands seems to me to open the way to a vast inflation of the currency. "'I had hoped to support this bill, but I cannot vote for it cause it seems to me to contain features and to rest upon principles in the highest degree menacing to our prosperity, to stability in business, and to the general welfare of the people of the United States.

Very Truly Yours,

Henry Cabot Lodge.'"

"In eighteen years that have passed since Senator Lodge wrote that letter of warning all of his predictions have come true. The Government is in the banking business as never before. Against its will it has been made the backer of horse thieves and card sharps, bootlegger's smugglers, speculators, and swindlers in all parts of the world. Through the Fed the riffraff of every country is operating on the public credit of the United States Government.

THE GREAT DEPRESSION

"Meanwhile and on account of it, we ourselves are in the midst of the greatest depression we have ever known. From the Atlantic to the Pacific, our Country has been ravaged and laid waste by the evil practices of the Fed and the interests which control them. At no time in our history, has the general welfare of the people been at a lower level or the minds of the people so full of despair.

"Recently in one of our States, 60,000 dwelling houses and farms were brought under the hammer in a single day. 71,000 houses and farms in Oakland County, Michigan, were sold and their erstwhile owners dispossessed. The people who have thus been driven out are the wastage of the Fed. They are the victims of the Fed. Their children are the new slaves of the auction blocks in the revival of the institution of human slavery.

The Scheme of the Fed

"In 1913, before the Senate Banking and Currency Committee, Mr. Alexander Lassen made the following statement: "The whole scheme of the Fed with its commercial paper is an impractical, cumbersome machinery- is simply a cover to secure the privilege of issuing money, and to evade payment of as much tax upon circulation as possible and then control the issue and maintain, instead of reducing interest rates. It will prove to the advantage of the few and the detriment of the people. It will mean continued shortage of actual money and further extension of credits, for when there is a shortage of money people have to borrow to their cost.' "A few days before the Fed passed, Senator Root denounced the Fed as an outrage on our liberties. He predicted: 'Long before we wake up from our dream of prosperity through an inflated currency, our gold- which alone could have kept us from catastrophe- will have vanished and no rate of interest will tempt it to return.'

"If ever a prophecy came true, that one did.

"The Fed became law the day before Christmas Eve, in the year 1913, and shortly afterwards, the German International bankers, Kuhn, Loeb and Co. sent one of their partners here to run it.

"The Fed Note is essentially unsound. It is the worst currency and the most dangerous that this Country has ever known. When the proponents of the act saw that the Democratic doctrine would not permit them to let the proposed banks issue the new currency as bank notes, they should have stopped at that. They should not have foisted that kind of currency, namely, an asset currency, on the United States Government. They should not have made the Government [liable on the private] debts of individuals and corporations, and, least of all, on the private debts of foreigners. "As Kemerer says: 'The Fed Notes, therefore, in form, have some of the qualities of Government paper money, but in substance, are almost a pure asset currency possessing a Government guarantee against which contingency the Government has made no provision whatever.'

"Hon. L.J.Hill, a former member of the House, said, and truly: "They are obligations of the Government for which the United States received nothing and for the payment of which at any time, it assumes the responsibility: looking to the Fed to recoup itself.'

"If this United States is to redeem the Fed Notes, when the General Public finds it costs to deliver this paper to the Fed, and if the Government has made no provisions for redeeming them, the first element of unsoundness is not far to seek.

"Before the Banking and Currency Committee, when the bill was under discussion Mr. Crozier of Cincinnati said: 'The imperial power of elasticity of the public currency is wielded exclusively by the central corporations owned by the banks. This is a life and death power over all local banks and all business. It can be used to create or destroy prosperity, to ward off or cause stringencies and panics. By making money artificially scarce, interest rates throughout the Country can be arbitrarily raised and the bank tax on all business and cost of living increased for the profit of the banks owning these regional central banks, and without the slightest benefit to the people. The 12 Corporations together cover y and monopolize and use for private gain- every dollar of the public currency and all public revenue of the United States. Not a dollar can be put into circulation among the people by their Government, without the consent of and on terms fixed by these 12 private money trusts.'

"In defiance of this and all other warnings, the proponents of the Fed created the 12 private credit corporations and gave them an absolute monopoly of the currency of these United States- not of the Fed Notes alone- but of all other currency! The Fed Act providing ways and means by which the gold and general currency in the hands of the American people could be obtained by the Fed in exchange for Fed Notes- which are not money- but mere promises to pay.

"Since the evil day when this was done, the initial monopoly has been extended by vicious amendments to the Fed and by the unlawful and treasonable practices of the Fed.

Money for the Scottish Distillers

"Mr. Chairman, if a Scottish distiller wishes to send a cargo of Scotch whiskey to these United States, he can draw his bill against the purchasing bootlegger in dollars and after the bootlegger has accepted it by writing his name across the face of it, the Scotch distiller can send that bill to the nefarious open discount market in New York City where the Fed will buy it and use it as collateral for a new issue of Fed Notes. Thus the Government of these United States pay the Scotch distiller for the whiskey before it is shipped, and if it is lost on the way, or if the Coast Guard seizes it and destroys it, the Fed simply write off the loss and the government never recovers the money that was paid to the Scotch distiller.

"While we are attempting to enforce prohibition here, the Fed are in the distillery business in Europe and paying bootlegger bills with public credit of these United States. "Mr. Chairman, by the same process, they compel our Government to pay the German brewer for his beer. Why should the Fed be permitted to finance the brewing industry in Germany either in this way or as they do by compelling small and fearful United States Banks to take stock in the Isenbeck Brewery and in the German Bank for brewing industries? "Mr. Chairman, if Dynamit Nobel of Germany, wishes to sell dynamite in Japan to use in Manchuria or elsewhere, it can drew its bill against the Japanese customers in dollars and send that bill to the nefarious open discount market in New York City where the Fed will buy it and use it as collateral for a new issue of Fed Notes- while at the same time the Fed will be helping Dynamit Nobel by stuffing its stock into the United States banking system.

"Why should we send our representatives to the disarmament conference at Geneva- while the Fed is making our Government pay Japanese debts to German Munitions makers?

"Mr. Chairman, if a German wishes to raise a crop of beans and sell them to a Japanese customer, he can draw a bill against his prospective Japanese customer in dollars and have it purchased by the Fed and get the money out of this Country at the expense of the American people before he has even planted the beans in the ground. "Mr. Chairman, if a German in Germany wishes to export goods to South America, or any other Country, he can draw his bill against his customers and send it to these United States and get the money out of this Country before he ships, or even manufactures the goods.

"Mr. Chairman, why should the currency of these United States be issued on the strength of German Beer? Why should it be issued on the crop of unplanted beans to be grown in Chili for Japanese consumption? Why should these United States be compelled to issue many billions of dollars every year to pay the debts of one foreigner to another foreigner? "Was it for this that our National Bank depositors had their money taken out of our banks and shipped abroad? Was it for this that they had to lose it? Why should the public credit of these United States and likewise money belonging to our National Bank depositors be used to support foreign brewers, narcotic drug vendors, whiskey distillers, wig makes, human hair merchants, Chilean bean growers, to finance the munition factories of Germany and Soviet Russia?

THE UNITED STATES HAS BEEN RANSACKED

"The United States has been ransacked and pillaged. Our structures have been gutted and only the walls are left standing. While being perpetrated, everything the world would rake up to sell us was brought in here at our expense by the Fed until our markets were swamped with unneeded and unwanted imported goods priced far above their value and make to equal the dollar volume of our honest exports, and to kill or reduce our favorite balance of trade. As Agents of the foreign central banks the Fed try by every means in their power to reduce our favorable balance of trade. They act for their foreign principal and they accept fees from foreigners for acting against the best interests of these United States. Naturally there has been great competition among among foreigners for the favors of the Fed.

"What we need to do is to send the reserves of our National Banks home to the people who earned and produced them and who still own them and to the banks which were compelled to surrender them to predatory interests.

"Mr. Chairman, there is nothing like the Fed pool of confiscated bank deposits in the world. It is a public trough of American wealth in which the foreigners claim rights, equal to or greater than Americans. The Fed are the agents of the foreign central banks. They use our bank depositors' money for the benefit of their foreign principals. They barter the public credit of the United States Government and hire it our to foreigners at a profit to themselves.

"All this is done at the expense of the United States Government, and at a sickening loss to the American people. Only our great wealth enabled us to stand the drain of it as long as we did.

"We need to destroy the Fed wherein our national reserves are impounded for the benefit of the foreigners. "We need to save America for Americans.

SPURIOUS SECURITIES

"Mr. Chairman, when you hold a $10.00 Fed Note in your hand, you are holding apiece of paper which sooner or later is going to cost the United States Government $10.00 in gold (unless the Government is obliged to go off the gold standard). It is based on limburger cheese (reported to be in foreign warehouses) or in cans purported to contain peas (but may contain salt water instead), or horse meat, illicit drugs, bootleggers fancies, rags and bones from Soviet Russia (of which these United States imported over a million dollars worth last year), on wines whiskey, natural gas, goat and dog fur, garlic on the string, and Bombay ducks.

"If you like to have paper money- which is secured by such commodities- you have it in Fed Note. If you desire to obtain the thing of value upon which this paper currency is based, that is, the limburger cheese, the whiskey, the illicit drugs, or any of the other staples- you will have a ⁓y hard time finding them.

⁓ᵗhese worshipful commodities are in foreign Countries. Are you going to Germany to ⁓rehouses to see if the specified things of value are there? I think more, I do not ⁓ld find them there if you did go.

"On April 27, 1932, the Fed outfit sent $750,000 belonging to American bank depositors in gold to Germany. A week later another $300,000 in gold was shipped to Germany. About the middle of May $12,000,000 in gold was shipped to Germany by the Fed. Almost every week there is a shipment of gold to Germany. These shipments are not made for profit on the exchange since the German marks are blow parity with the dollar.

"Mr. Chairman, I believe that the National Bank depositors of these United States have a right to know what the Fed are doing with their money. There are millions of National Bank depositors in the Country who do not know that a percentage of every dollar they deposit in a Member Bank of the Fed goes automatically to American Agents of the foreign banks and that all their deposits can be paid away to foreigners without their knowledge or consent by the crooked machinery of the Fed and the questionable practices of the Fed.

[Ed. Note- Problem with next paragraph in original] "Mr. Chairman, the American people should be told the truth by their servants in office. In 1930, we had over a half billion dollars outstanding daily to finance foreign goods stored in or shipped between several billion dollars. What goods are these on which the Fed yearly pledge several billions of dollars. In its yearly total, this item amounts to several billions of dollars of the public credit of these United States?

"What goods are those which are hidden in European and Asiatic stores have not been seen by any officer of our Government but which are being financed on the public credit of the United States Government? What goods are those upon which the 17 United States Government is being obligated by the Fed to issue Fed Notes to the extent of several billions of dollars a year?

The Bankers' Acceptance Racket

"The Fed have been International Banks from the beginning, with these United States as their enforced banker and supplier of currency. But it is none the less extraordinary to see these these twelve private credit monopolies, buying the debts of foreigners against foreigners, in all parts of the world and asking the Government of these United States for new issues of Fed notes in exchange for them. "The magnitude of the acceptance racket as it has been developed by the Fed, their foreign correspondents, and the predatory European born bankers, who set up the Fed here and taught your own, by and of pirates, how to loot the people: I say the magnitude of this racket is estimated to be in the neighborhood of 9,000,000,000 per year. In the past ten years it is said to have amounted to $90,000,000,000.00. In my opinion it has amounted to several times that much. coupled to this you have to the extent of billions of dollars, the gambling in the United States securities, which takes place in the same open discount market- a gambling on which the Fed is now spending $100,000,000.00 per week.

"Fed Notes are taken from the U.S. Government in unlimited quantities. Is is strange that the burden of supplying these immense sums of money to the gambling fraternity has at last proved too heavy for the American people to endure? Would it not be a national [calamity to] again bind down this burden on the backs of the American people and by means of a long rawhide whip of the credit masters, compel them to enter another seventeen years of slavery?

"They are trying to do that now. They are trying to take $100,000,000.00 of the public credit of the United States every week, in addition to all their other seizures and they are sending that money to the nefarious open market in a desperate gamble to reestablish their graft as a going concern.

"They are putting the United States Government in debt to the extent of $100,000,000 a week, and with the money they are buying our Government securities for themselves and their foreign principals. Our people are disgusted with the experiences of the Fed. The Fed is not producing a loaf of bread, a yard of cloth, a bushel of corn, or a pile of cordwood by its check-kiting operations in the money market.

"Mr. Speaker, on the 13th of January of this year I addressed the House on the subject of the Reconstruction Finance Corporation. In the course of my remarks I made the following statement: In 1928 the member banks of the Fed borrowed $60,598,690,000. from the Fed on their fifteen-day promissory notes. Think of it. Sixty billion dollars payable on demand in gold in the course of one single year. The actual amount of such obligations called for six times as much monetary gold as there is in the world. Such transactions represent a grant in the course of one single years of about $7,000,000 to every member of the Fed.

"Is it any wonder that American labor which ultimately pays the cost of all banking operations of this Country has at last proved unequal to the task of supplying this huge total of cash and credit for the benefit of the stock market manipulators and foreign swindlers? "In 1933 the Fed presented the staggering amount of $60,598,690,000 to its member banks at the expense of the wage earners and tax payers of these United States. In 1929, the year of the stock market crash, the Fed advanced $58,000,000,000 to member banks.

"In 1930 while the speculating banks were getting out of the stock market at the expense of the general public, the Fed advanced them $13,022,782,000. This shows that when the banks were gambling on the public credit of these United States as represented by the Fed currency they were subsidized to any amount they required by the Fed. When the swindle began to fall, the bankers knew it in advance and withdrew from the market. They got out with whole skins- and left the people of these United States to pay the piper. "My friend from Kansas, Mr. McGugin, has stated that he thought the Fed lent money on rediscounting. So they do, but they lend comparatively little that way. The real discounting that they do has been called a mere penny in the slot business. It is too slow for genuine high flyers. They discourage it. They prefer to subsidize their favorite banks by making them $60,000,000,000 advances and they prefer to acquire assistance in the notorious open discount market in New York, where they can use it to control the price of stocks and bonds on the exchanges.

"For every dollar they advanced on discounts in 1928, they lent $33.00 to their favorite banks for whom they do a business of several billion dollars income tax on their profits to these United States.

The John Law Swindle

"This is the John Law swindle over again. The theft of Teapot Dome was trifling compared to it. What King ever robbed his subject to such an extent as the Fed has robbed us? Is it any wonder that there have been lately ninety cases of starvation in one of the New York hospitals? Is there any wonder that the children are being abandoned?

"The government and the people of these United States have been swindled by swindlers deluxe to whom the acquisition of American or a parcel of Fed Notes presented no more difficulty than the drawing up of a worthless acceptance in a Country not subject to the laws of these United States, by sharpers not subject to the jurisdiction of these United States, sharpers with strong banking "fence" on this side of the water, a "fence" acting as a receiver of a worthless paper coming from abroad, endorsing it and getting the currency out of the Fed for it as quickly as possible exchanging that currency for gold and in turn transmitting the gold to its foreign confederates.

Ivar Kreuger, the Match King!

"Such were the exploits of Ivar Krueger, Mr. Hoover's friend, and his rotten Wall Street bakers. Every dollar of the billions Kreuger and his gang drew out of this Country on acceptances was drawn from the government and the people of the United States through the Fed. The credit of the United States Government was peddled to him by the Fed for their own private gain. That is what the Fed has been doing for many years.

"They have been peddling the credit of this Government and the [signature of this] Government to the swindlers and speculators of all nations. That is what happens when a Country forsakes its Constitution and gives its sovereignty over the public currency to private interests. Give them the flag and they will sell it.

"The nature of Kreuger's organized swindle and the bankrupt condition of Kreuger's combine was known here last June when Hoover sought to exempt Krueger's loan to Germany of $125,000,000 from the operation of the Hoover Moratorium. The bankrupt condition of Krueger's swindle was known her last summer when $30,000,000 was taken from the American taxpayers by certain bankers in New York for the ostensible purpose of permitting Krueger to make a loan to Colombia. Colombia never saw that money.

"The nature of Krueger's swindle was known here in January when he visited his friend, Mr. Hoover, at the White House. It was known here in March before he went to Paris and committed suicide.

"Mr. Chairman, I think the people of the United States are entitled to know how many billions of dollars were placed at the disposal of Krueger and his gigantic combine by the Fed, and to know how much of our Government currency was issued and lost in the financing of that great swindle in the years during which the Fed took care of Krueger's requirements.

"A few days ago, the President of the United States with a white face and shaking hands, went before the Senate of behalf of the moneyed interests and asked the Senate to levy a tax on the people so that foreigners might know that these United States would pay its debt to them.

"Most Americans thought it was the other way around. What does these United States owe foreigners? When and by whom was the debt incurred? It was incurred by the Fed, when they peddled the signature of the Government to foreigners- for a Price. It is what the United States Government has to pay to redeem the obligations of the Fed.

Thieves Go Scot Free

"Are you going to let these thieves get off scot free? Is there one law for the looter who drives up to the door of the United States Treasury in his limousine and another for the United States Veterans who are sleeping on the floor of a dilapidated house on the outskirts of Washington?

"The Baltimore and Ohio Railroad is here asking for a large loan from the people, and the wage earners and the taxpayers of these United States. It is begging for a handout from the Government. It is standing, cap in hand, at the door of the R.F.C. where all the jackals have gathered to the feast. It is asking for money that was raised from the people by taxation and wants this money of the poor for the benefit of Kuhn, Loeb and Co., the German International Bankers.

"Is there one law for the Baltimore and Ohio Railroad and another for the hungry veterans it threw off its freight cars the other day? Is there one law for sleek and prosperous swindlers who call themselves bankers and another law for the soldiers who defended the flag? "The R.F.C. is taking over these worthless securities from the Investment Trusts with United States Treasury money at the expense of the American taxpayer and the wage earner.

"It will take twenty years to redeem our Government. Twenty years of penal servitude to pay off the gambling debts of the traitorous Fed and to vast flood of American wages and savings, bank deposits, and the United States Government credit which the Fed exported out of this country to their foreign principals.

"The Fed lately conducted an anti-hoarding campaign here. They they took that extra money which they had persuaded the American people to put into the banks- they sent it to Europe- along with the rest. In the last several months, they have sent $1,300,000,000 in gold to their foreign employers, their foreign masters, and every dollar of that gold belonged to the people of these United States and was unlawfully taken from them.

Fiat Money

"Mr. Chairman, within the limits of the time allowed me, I cannot enter into a particularized discussion of the Fed. I have singled out the Fed currency for a few remarks because there has lately been some talk here of "fiat money". What kind of money is being pumped into the open discount market and through it into foreign channels and stock exchanges? Mr. Mills of the Treasury has spoken here of his horror of the printing presses and his horror of dishonest money. He has no horror of dishonest money. If he had, he would be no party to the present gambling of the Fed in the nefarious open discount market of New York, a market in which the sellers are represented by 10 discount corporations owned and organized by the very banks which own and control the Fed.

"Fiat money, indeed!

"What Mr. Mills is fighting for is the preservation, whole and entire, of the banker's monopoly of all the currency of the United States Government.

"Mr. Chairman, last December, I introduced a resolution here asking for an examination and an audit of the Fed and all related matters. If the House sees fit to make such an investigation, the people of these United States will obtain information of great value. This is a Government of the people, by the people, for the people. Consequently, nothing should be concealed from the people. The man who deceives the people is a traitor to these United States.

"The man who knows or suspects that a crime has been committed and who conceals and covers up that crime is an accessory to it. Mr. Speaker, it is a monstrous thing for this great nation of people to have its destinies presided over by a traitorous government board acting in secret concert with international usurers.

"Every effort has been made by the Fed to conceal its powers- but the truth is- the Fed has usurped the Government. It controls everything here and it controls all of our foreign relations. It makes and breaks governments at will.

"No man and no body of men is more entrenched in power than the arrogant credit monopoly which operated the Fed. What National Government has permitted the Fed to steal from the people should now be restored to the people. The people have a valid claim against the Fed. If that claim is enforced the Americans will not need to stand in the bread line, or to suffer and die of starvation in the streets. Women will be saved, families will be kept together, and American children will not be dispersed and abandoned.

"Here is a Fed Note. Immense numbers of the notes are now held abroad. I am told that they amount to upwards of a billion dollars. They constitute a claim against our Government and likewise a claim against our peoples' money to the extent of $1,300,000,000 which has within the last few months been shipped abroad to redeem Fed Notes and to pay other gambling debts of the traitorous Fed. The greater part of our money stock has been shipped to other lands.

"Why should we promise to pay the debts of foreigners to foreigners? Why should the Fed be permitted to finance our competitors in all parts of the world? Do you know why the tariff was raised? It was raised to shut out the flood of Fed Goods pouring in here from every quarter of the globe- cheap goods, produced by cheaply paid foreign labor, on unlimited supplies of money and credit sent out of this Country by the dishonest and unscrupulous Fed.

"The Fed are spending $100,000,000 a week buying government securities in the open market and are making a great bid for foreign business. They are trying to make rates so attractive that the human hair merchants and the distillers and other business entities in foreign land will come her and hire more of the public credit of the United States Government to pay the Fed outfit for getting it for them.

World Enslavement Planned

"Mr. Chairman, when the Fed was passed, the people of these United States did not perceive that a world system was being set up here which would make the savings of the American school teacher available to a narcotic-drug vendor in Acapulco. They did not perceive that these United States was to be lowered to the position of a coolie country which has nothing but raw material and heart, that Russia was destined to supply the man power and that this country was to supply the financial power to an "international superstate". A superstate controlled by international bankers, and international industrialists acting together to enslave the world for their own pleasure?

"The people of these United States are being greatly wronged. They have been driven from their employments. They have been dispossessed from their homes. They have been evicted from their rented quarters. They have lost their children. They have been left to suffer and die for lack of shelter, food, clothing and medicine.

"The wealth of these United States and the working capital have been taken away from them and has either been locked in the vaults of certain banks and the great corporations or exported to foreign countries for the benefit of the foreign customers of these banks and corporations. So far as the people of the United States are concerned, the cupboard is bare.

"It is true that the warehouses and coal yards and grain elevators are full, but these are padlocked, and the great banks and corporations hold the keys.

"The sack of these United States by the Fed is the greatest crime in history.

"Mr. Chairman, a serious situation confronts the House of Representatives today. We are trustees of the people and the rights of the people are being taken away from them. Through the Fed the people are losing the rights guaranteed to them by the Constitution. Their property has been taken from them without due process of law. Mr. Chairman, common decency requires us to examine the public accounts of the Government and see what crimes against the public welfare have been committed.

"What is needed here is a return to the Constitution of these United States.

"The old struggle that was fought out here in Jackson's time must be fought our over again. The independent United States Treasury should be reestablished and the Government should keep its own money under lock and key in the building the people provided for that purpose.

"Asset currency, the devise of the swindler, should be done away with. The Fed should be abolished and the State boundaries should be respected. Bank reserves should be kept within the boundaries of the States whose people own them, and this reserve money of the people should be protected so that the International Bankers and acceptance bankers and discount dealers cannot draw it away from them.

"The Fed should be repealed, and the Fed Banks, having violated their charters, should be liquidated immediately. Faithless Government officials who have violated their oaths of office should be impeached and brought to trial.

"Unless this is done by us, I predict, that the American people, outraged, pillaged, insulted and betrayed as they are in their own land, will rise in their wrath, and will sweep the money changers out of the temple.
"Mr. Chairman, the United States is bankrupt: It has been bankrupted by the corrupt and dishonest Fed. It has repudiated its debts to its own citizens. Its chief foreign creditor is Great

Britain, and a British bailiff has been at the White House and the British Agents are in the United States Treasury making inventory arranging terms of liquidations!

Great Britain, Partner in Blackmail

"Mr. Chairman, the Fed has offered to collect the British claims in full from the American public by trickery and corruption, if Great Britain will help to conceal its crimes. The British are shielding their agents, the Fed, because they do not wish that system of robbery to be destroyed here. They wish it to continue for their benefit! By means of it, Great Britain has become the financial mistress of the world. She has regained the position she occupied before the World War.

"For several years she has been a silent partner in the business of the Fed. Under threat of blackmail, or by their bribery, or by their native treachery to the people of the United States, the officials in charge of the Fed unwisely gave Great Britain immense gold loans running into hundreds of millions of dollars. They did this against the law! Those gold loans were not single transactions. They gave Great Britain a borrowing power in the United States of billions. She squeezed billions out of this Country by means of her control of the Fed.

"As soon as the Hoover Moratorium was announced, Great Britain moved to consolidate her gains. After the treacherous signing away of American rights at the 7-power conference at London in July, 1931, which put the Fed under the control of the Bank of International Settlements, Great Britain began to tighten the hangman's noose around the neck of the United States.

"She abandoned the gold standard and embarked on a campaign of buying up the claims of foreigners against the Fed in all parts of the world. She has now sent her bailiff, Ramsey MacDonald, here to get her war debt to this country canceled. But she has a club in her hands! She has title to the gambling debts which the corrupt and dishonest Fed incurred abroad.

"Ramsey MacDonald, the labor party deserter, has come here to compel the President to sign on the dotted line, and that is what Roosevelt is about to do! Roosevelt will endeavor to conceal the nature of his action from the American people. But he will obey the International Bankers and transfer the war debt that Great Britain should pay to the American people, to the shoulders of the American taxpayers.

"Mr. Chairman, the bank holiday in the several States was brought about by the corrupt and dishonest Fed. These institutions manipulated money and credit, and caused the States to order bank holidays.

"These holidays were frame-ups! "They were dress rehearsals for the national bank holiday which Franklin D. Roosevelt promised Sir Ramsey MacDonald that he would declare.

"There was no national emergency here when Franklin D. Roosevelt took office excepting the bankruptcy of the Fed- a bankruptcy which has been going on under cover for several years and which has been concealed from the people so that the people would continue to permit their bank deposits and their bank reserves and their gold and the funds of the United States Treasury to be impounded in these bankrupt institutions.

"Under cover, the predatory International Bankers have been stealthily transferring the burden of the Fed debts to the people's Treasury and to the people themselves. They the farms and the homes of the United States to pay for their thievery! That is the only national emergency that there has been here since the depression began.

"The week before the bank holiday ws declared in New York State, the deposits in the New York savings banks were greater than the withdrawals. There were no runs on New York Banks. There was no need of a bank holiday in New York, or of a national holiday.

Roosevelt and the International Bankers

"Roosevelt did what the International Bankers ordered him to do!

"Do not deceive yourself, Mr. Chairman, or permit yourself to be deceived by others into the belief that Roosevelt's dictatorship is in any way intended to benefit the people of the United States: he is preparing to sign on the dotted line! "He is preparing to cancel the war debts by fraud!

"He is preparing to internationalize this Country and to destroy our Constitution itself in order to keep the Fed intact as a money institution for foreigners. "Mr. Chairman, I see no reason why citizens of the United States should be terrorized into surrendering their property to the International Bankers who own and control the Fed. The statement that gold would be taken from its lawful owners if they did not voluntarily surrender it, to private interests, show that there is an anarchist in our Government.

"The statement that it is necessary for the people to give their gold- the only real money- to the banks in order to protect the currency, is a statement of calculated dishonesty!

"By his unlawful usurpation of power on the night of March 5, 1933, and by his proclamation, which in my opinion was in violation of the Constitution of the United States, Roosevelt divorced the currency of the United States from gold, and the United States currency is no longer protected by gold. It is therefore sheer dishonesty to say that the people's gold is needed to protect the currency.

"Roosevelt ordered the people to give their gold to private interests- that is, to banks, and he took control of the banks so that all the gold and gold values in them, or given into them, might be handed over to the predatory International Bankers who own and control the Fed.

"Roosevelt cast his lot with the usurers. "He agreed to save the corrupt and dishonest at the expense of the people of the United States.

"He took advantage of the people's confusion and weariness and spread the dragnet over the United States to capture everything of value that was left in it. He made a great haul for the International Bankers.

"The Prime Minister of England came here for money! He came here to collect cash!

"He came here with Fed Currency and other claims against the Fed which England had bought up in all parts of the world. And he has presented them for redemption in gold.

"Mr. Chairman, I am in favor of compelling the Fed to pay their own debts. I see no reason why the general public should be forced to pay the gambling debts of the International Bankers.

Roosevelt Seizes the Gold

"By his action in closing the banks of the United States, Roosevelt seized the gold value of forty billions or more of bank deposits in the United States banks. Those deposits were deposits of gold values. By his action he has rendered them payable to the depositors in paper only, if payable at all, and the paper money he proposes to pay out to bank depositors and to the people generally in lieu of their hard earned gold values in itself, and being based on nothing into which the people can convert it the said paper money is of negligible value altogether.

"It is the money of slaves, not of free men. If the people of the United States permit it to be imposed upon them at the will of their credit masters, the next step in their downward progress will be their acceptance of orders on company stores for what they eat and wear. Their case will be similar to that of starving coal miners. They, too, will be paid with orders on Company stores for food and clothing, both of indifferent quality and be forced to live in Company-owned houses from which they may be evicted at the drop of a hat. More of them will be forced into conscript labor camps under supervision.

"At noon on the 4th of March, 1933, FDR with his hand on the Bible, took an oath to preserve, protect and defend the Constitution of the U.S. At midnight on the 5th of March, 1933, he confiscated the property of American citizens. He took the currency of the United States standard of value. He repudiated the internal debt of the Government to its own citizens. He destroyed the value of the American dollar. He released, or endeavored to release, the Fed from their contractual liability to redeem Fed currency in gold or lawful money on a parity with gold. He depreciated the value of the national currency.

"The people of the U.S. are now using unredeemable paper slips for money. The Treasury cannot redeem that paper in gold or silver. The gold and silver of the Treasury has unlawfully been given to the corrupt and dishonest Fed. And the Administration has since had the effrontery to raid the country for more gold for the private interests by telling our patriotic citizens that their gold is needed to protect the currency.

"It is not being used to protect the currency! It is being used to protect the corrupt and dishonest Fed. "The directors of these institutions have committed criminal offense against the United States Government, including the offense of making false entries on their books, and the still more serious offense of unlawfully abstracting funds from the United States Treasury! "Roosevelt's gold raid is intended to help them out of the pit they dug for themselves when they gambled away the wealth and savings of the American people.

Dictatorship

"The International Bankers set up a dictatorship here because they wanted a dictator who would protect them. They wanted a dictator who would protect them. They wanted a dictator who would issue a proclamation giving the Fed an absolute and unconditional release from their special currency in gold, or lawful money of any Fed Bank.

"Has Roosevelt relieved any other class of debtors in this country from the necessity of paying their debts? Has he made a proclamation telling the farmers that they need not pay their mortgages? Has he made a proclamation to the effect that mothers of starving children need not pay their milk bills? Has he made a proclamation relieving householders from the necessity of paying rent?

Roosevelt's Two Kinds of Laws

"Not he! He has issued one kind of proclamation only, and that is a proclamation to relieve international bankers and the foreign debtors of the United States Government.

"Mr. Chairman, the gold in the banks of this country belongs to the American people who have paper money contracts for it in the form of national currency. If the Fed cannot keep their contracts with United States citizens to redeem their paper money in gold, or lawful money, then the Fed must be taken over by the United States Government and their officers must be put on trial.

"There must be a day of reckoning. If the Fed have looted the Treasury so that the Treasury cannot redeem the United States currency for which it is liable in gold, then the Fed must be driven out of the Treasury.

"Mr. Chairman, a gold certificate is a warehouse receipt for gold in the Treasury, and the man who has a gold certificate is the actual owner of a corresponding amount of gold stacked in the Treasury subject to his order.

"Now comes Roosevelt who seeks to render the money of the United States worthless by unlawfully declaring that it may No Longer be converted into gold at the will of the holder.

"Roosevelt's next haul for the International Bankers was the reduction in the pay of all Federal employees.

"Next in order are the veterans of all wars, many of whom are aged and inform, and other sick and disabled. These men had their lives adjusted for them by acts of Congress determining the amounts of the pensions, and, while it is meant that every citizen should sacrifice himself for the good of the United States, I see no reason why those poor people, these aged Civil War Veterans and war widows and half-starved veterans of the World War, should be compelled to give up their pensions for the financial benefit of the International vultures who have looted the Treasury, bankrupted the country and traitorously delivered the United States to a foreign foe.

"There are many ways of raising revenue that are better than that barbaric act of injustice.

"Why not collect from the Fed the amount they owe the U.S. Treasury in interest on all the Fed currency they have taken from the Government? That would put billions of dollars into the U.S. Treasury.

"If FDR is as honest as he pretends to be, he will have that done immediately. And in addition, why not compel the Fed to disclose their profits and to pay the Government its share?

"Until this is done, it is rank dishonesty to talk of maintaining the credit of the U.S. Government. "My own salary as a member of Congress has been reduced, and while I am willing to give my part of it that has been taken away from me to the U.S. Government, I regret that the U.S. has suffered itself to be brought so low by the vultures and crooks who are operating the roulette wheels and faro tables in the Fed, that is now obliged to throw itself on the mercy of its legislators and charwomen, its clerks, and it poor pensioners and to take money out of our pockets to make good the defalcations of the International Bankers who were placed in control of the Treasury and given the monopoly of U.S. Currency by the misbegotten Fed. "I am well aware that the International Bankers who drive up to the door of the United States Treasury in their limousines, look down with scorn upon members of Congress because we work for so little, while they draw millions a year. The difference is that we earn, or try to earn, what we get- and they steal the greater part of their takings.

Enemies of the People They Rob

"I do not like to see vivisections performed on human beings. I do not like to see the American people used for experimental purposes by the credit masters of the United States. They predicted among themselves that they would be able to produce a condition here in which American citizens would be completely humbled and left starving and penniless in the streets.

"The fact that they made that assertion while they were fomenting their conspiracy against the United States that they like to see a human being, especially an American, stumbling from hunger when he walks. "Something should be done about it, they say. Five-cent meals, or something! "But FDR will not permit the House of Representatives to investigate the condition of the Fed. FDR will not do that. He has certain International Bankers to serve. They not look to him as the man Higher Up who will protect them from the just wrath of an outraged people.

"The International Bankers have always hated our pensioners. A man with a small pension is a ward of the Government. He is not dependent upon them for a salary or wages. They cannot control him. They do not like him. It gave them great pleasure, therefore, to slash the veterans.

"But FDR will never do anything to embarrass his financial supporters. He will cover up the crimes of the Fed.
"Before he was elected, Mr. Roosevelt advocated a return to the earlier practices of the Fed, thus admitting its corruptness. The Democratic platform advocated a change in the personnel of the Fed. These were campaign bait. As a prominent Democrat lately remarked to me; "There is no new deal. The same old crowd is in control."

"The claims of foreign creditors of the Fed have no validity in law. The foreign creditors were the receivers- and the willing receivers- of stolen goods! They have received through their banking fences immense amounts of currency, and that currency was unlawfully taken from the United States Treasury by the Fed.

"England discovered the irregularities of the Fed quite early in its operations and through fear, apparently, the Fed have for years suffered themselves to be blackmailed and dragooning England to share in the business of the Fed. "The Fed have unlawfully taken many millions of dollars of the public credit of the United States and have given it to foreign sellers on the security of the Debt paper of foreign buyers in purely foreign transactions, and when the foreign buyers refused to meet their obligations and the Fed saw no honest way of getting the stolen goods back into their possession, they decided by control of the executive to make the American people pay their losses!

Conspiracy of War Debts

"They likewise entered into a conspiracy to deprive the people of the U.S. of their title to the war debts and not being able to do that in the way they intended, they are now engaged in an effort to debase the American dollar so that foreign governments will have their debts to this country cut in two, and then by means of other vicious underhanded arrangements, they propose to remit the remainder.

"So far as the U.S. is concerned, the gambling counters have no legal standing. The U.S. Treasury cannot be compelled to make good the gambling ventures of the corrupt and dishonest Fed. Still less should the bank deposits of the U.S. be used for that purpose. Still less should the national currency have been made irredeemable in gold so that the gold which was massed and stored to redeem the currency for American citizens may be used to pay the gambling debts of the Fed for England's benefit. "The American people should have their gold in their own possession where it cannot be held under secret agreement for any foreign control bank, or world bank, or foreign nation. Our own citizens have the prior claim to it. The paper [money men] have in their possession deserves redemption far more than U.S. currency and credit which was stolen from the U.S. Treasury and bootlegged abroad.

"Why should the foreigners be made preferred creditors of the bankrupt U.S.? Why should the U.S. be treated as bankrupt at all? This Government has immense sums due it from the Fed. The directors of these institutions are men of great wealth. Why should the guilty escape the consequences of their misdeeds? Why should the people of these U.S. surrender the value of their gold bank deposits to pay off the gambling debts of these bankers? Why should Roosevelt promise foreigners that the U.S. will play the part of a good neighbor, 'meeting its obligations'?

"Let the Fed meet their own obligations.
"Every member of the Fed should be compelled to disgorge, and every acceptance banker and every discount corporation which has made illegal profits by means of public credit unlawfully bootlegged out of the U.S. Treasury and hired out by the crooks and vultures of the Fed should be compelled to disgorge.

Federal Reserve Pays No Taxes

"Gambling debts due to foreign receivers of stolen goods should not be paid by sacrificing our title to our war debts, the assets of the U.S. Treasury- which belong to all the people of the U.S. and which it is our duty to preserve inviolate in the people's treasury.

"The U.S. Treasury cannot be made liable for them. The Fed currency must be redeemed by the Fed banks or else these Fed banks must be liquidated.

"We know from assertions made here by the Hon. John N. Garner, Vice-President of the U.S. that there is a condition in the [United States such] would cause American citizens, if they knew what it was, to lose all confidence in their government.

"That is a condition that Roosevelt will not have investigated. He has brought with him from Wall Street, James Warburg, the son of Paul M. Warburg. Mr. Warburg, alien born, and the son of an alien who did not become naturalized here until several years after this Warburg's birth, is a son of a former partner of Kuhn, Loeb and Co., a grandson of another partner, a nephew of a former partner, and a nephew of a present partner.

"He holds no office in our Government, but I am told that he is in daily attendance at the Treasury, and that he has private quarters there! In other words, Mr. Chairman, Kuhn, Loeb and Company now has control and occupy the U.S. Treasury.

Preferred Treatment for Foreigners

"The text of the Executive order which seems to place an embargo on shipments of gold permits the Secretary of the Treasury, a former director of the corrupt, to issue licenses at his discretion for the export of gold coin, or bullion, earmarked or held in trust for a recognized foreign government or foreign central bank for international settlement. Now, Mr. Chairman, if gold held in trust for those foreign institutions may be sent to them, I see no reason why gold held in trust for American as evidenced by their gold certificates and other currency issued by the U.S. Government should not be paid to them. "I think that American citizens should be entitled to treatment at least as good as that which the person is extending to foreign governments, foreign central banks, and the bank of International Settlements. I think a veteran of the world war, with a $20.00 gold certificate, is at least as much entitled to receive his own gold for it, as any international banker in the city of New York or London.

"By the terms of this executive order, gold may be exported if it is actually required, for the fulfillment of any contract entered into prior to the date of this order by an applicant who, in obedience to the executive order of April 5, 1933, has delivered gold coin, gold bullion, or gold certificates. "This means that gold may be exported to pay the obligations abroad of the Fed which were incurred prior to the date of the order, namely, April 20, 1933.

"If a European Bank should send 100,000,000 dollars in Fed currency to a bank in this country for redemption, that bank could easily ship gold to Europe in exchange for that currency. Such Fed currency would represent "contracts" entered into prior to the date of the order. If the Bank of International Settlements or any other foreign bank holding any of the present gambling debt paper of the Fed should draw a draft for the settlement of such obligation, gold would be shopped to them because the debt contract would have been entered into prior to the date of order.

Crimes and Criminals

"Mr. Speaker, I rise to a question of constitutional privilege.

"Whereas, I charge. . .Eugene Meyer, Roy A. Young, Edmund Platt, Eugene B. Black, Adolph Casper Miller, Charles S. Hamlin, George R. James, Andrew W. Mellon, Ogden L. Mills, William H. Woo W. Poole, J.F.T. O'Connor, members of the Federal Reserve Board; F. H. Curtis, J.H. Chane, R.L. Austin, George De Camp, L.B. Williams, W.W. Hoxton, Oscar Newton, E.M. Stevens, J.S. Wood, J.N. Payton, M.L. McClure, C.C. Walsh, Isaac B. Newton, Federal Reserve Agents, jointly and severally, with violations of the Constitution and laws of the United States, and whereas I charge them with having taken funds from the U.S Treasury which were not appropriated by the Congress of the United States, and I charge them with having unlawfully taken over $80,000,000,000 from the U.S. Government in the year 1928, the said unlawful taking consisting of the unlawful creation of claims against the U.S. Treasury to the extent of over $80,000,000,000 in the year 1928; and I charge them with similar thefts committed in 1929, 1930, 1931, 1932 and 1933, and in years previous to 1928, amounting to billions of dollars; and

"Whereas I charge them, jointly and severally with having unlawfully created claims against the U.S. Treasury by unlawfully placing U.S. Government credit in specific amounts to the credit of foreign governments and foreign central banks of issue; private interests and commercial and private banks of the U.S. and foreign countries, and branches of foreign banks doing business in the U.S., to the extent of billions of dollars; and with having made unlawful contracts in the name of the U.S. Government and the U.S. Treasury; and with having made false entries on books of account; and

"Whereas I charge them jointly and severally, with having taken Fed Notes from the U.S. Treasury and with having put Fed Notes into circulation without obeying the mandatory provision of the Fed Act which requires the Fed Board to fix an interest rate on all issues of Fed Notes supplied to Fed Banks, the interest resulting therefrom to be paid by the Fed Banks to the government of the U.S. for the use of the Fed Notes, and I charge them of having defrauded the U.S. Government and the people of the U.S. of billions of dollars by the commission of this crime, and

"Whereas I charge them, jointly and severally, with having purchased U.S. Government securities with U.S. Government credit unlawfully taken and with having sold the said U.S. Government securities back to the people of the U.S. for gold or gold values and with having again purchased U.S. Government securities with U.S. Government credit unlawfully taken and with having again sold the said U.S. Government security for gold or gold values, and I charge them with having defrauded the U.S. Government and the people of the U.S. by this rotary process; and

"Whereas I charge them, jointly and severally, with having unlawfully negotiated U.S. Government securities, upon which the Government liability was extinguished, as collateral security for Fed Notes and with having substituted such securities for gold which was being held as collateral security for Fed Notes, and with having by the process defrauded the U.S. Government and the people of the U.S., and I charge them with the theft of all the gold and currency they obtained by this process; and

"Whereas I charge them, jointly and severally, with having unlawfully issued Fed currency on false, worthless and fictitious acceptances and other circulating evidence of debt, and with having made unlawful advances of Fed currency, and with having unlawfully permitted renewals of acceptances and renewals of other circulating evidences of debt, and with having permitted acceptance bankers and discount dealer corporations and other private bankers to violate the banking laws of the U.S.; and

"Whereas I charge them, jointly and severally, with having conspired to have evidences of debt to the extent of $1,000,000,000 artificially created at the end of February, 1933, and early in March 1933, and with having made unlawful issues and advances of Fed currency on the security of said artificially created evidences of debt for a sinister purpose, and with having assisted in the execution of said sinister purpose; and

"Whereas I charge them, jointly and severally, with having brought about the repudiation of the currency obligations of the Fed Banks to the people of the U.S. and with having conspired to obtain a release for the Fed Board and the Fed Banks from their contractual liability to redeem all Fed currency in gold or lawful money at the Fed Bank and with having defrauded the holders of Fed currency, and with having conspired to have the debts and losses of the Fed Board and the Fed Banks unlawfully transferred to the Government and the people of the U.S., and

"Whereas I charge them, jointly and severally, with having unlawfully substituted Fed currency and other irredeemable paper currency for gold in the hands of the people after the decision to repudiate the Fed currency and the national currency was made known to them, and with thus having obtained money under false pretenses; and

"Whereas I charge them, jointly and severally, with having brought about a repudiation of the notes of the U.S. in order that the gold value of the said currency might be given to private interests, foreign governments, foreign central banks of issues, and the Bank of International Settlements, and the people of the U.S. to be left without gold or lawful money and with no currency other that a paper currency irredeemable in gold, and I charge them with having done this for the benefit of private interests, foreign governments, foreign central banks of issue, and the bank of International Settlements; and

"Whereas I charge them, jointly and severally, with conniving with the Edge Law banks, and other Edge Law institutions, accepting banks, and discount corporations, foreign central banks of issue, foreign commercial banks, foreign corporations, and foreign individuals with funds unlawfully taken from the U.S. Treasury; and I charge them with having unlawfully permitted and made possible 'new financing' for foreigners at the expense of the U.S. Treasury to the extent of billions of dollars and with having unlawfully permitted and made possible the bringing into the United States of immense quantities of foreign securities, created in foreign countries for export to the U.S. and with having unlawfully permitted the said foreign securities to be imported into the U.S. instead of gold, which was lawfully due to the U.S. on trade balances and otherwise, and with having lawfully permitted and facilitated the sale of the said foreign securities in the U.S., and

"Whereas I charge them, jointly and severally, with having unlawfully exported U.S. coins and currency for a sinister purpose, and with having deprived the people of the U.S. of their lawful medium of exchange, and I charge them with having arbitrarily and unlawfully reduced the amount of money and currency in circulation in the U.S. to the lowest rate per capita in the history of the Government, so that the great mass of the people have been left without a sufficient medium of exchange, and I charge them with concealment and evasion in refusing to make known the amount of U.S. money in coins and paper currency exported and the amount remaining in the U.S. as a result of which refusal the Congress of the U.S. is unable to ascertain where the U.S. coins and issues of currency are at the present time, and what amount of U.S. currency is now held abroad; and

"Whereas I charge them, jointly and severally, with having arbitrarily and unlawfully raised and lowered the rates of money and with having arbitrarily increased and diminished the volume of currency in circulation for the benefit of private interests at the expense of the Government and the people of the U.S. and with having unlawfully manipulated money rates, wages, salaries and property values both real and personal, in the U.S. by unlawful operations in the open discount market and by resale and repurchase agreements unsanctioned by law, and

"Whereas I charge them jointly and severally, with having brought about the decline in prices on the New York Stock Exchange and other exchanges in October, 1929, by unlawful manipulation of money rates and the volume of U.S. money and currency in circulation: by theft of funds from the U.S. Treasury by gambling in acceptances and U.S. Government securities; by service rendered to foreign and domestic speculators and politicians, and by unlawful sale of U.S. gold reserves abroad, and

"Whereas the unconstitutional inflation law imbedded in the so-called Farm Relief Act by which the Fed Banks are given permission to buy U.S. Government securities to the extent of $3,000,000,000 and to drew forth currency from the people's Treasury to the extent of $3,000,000,000 is likely to result in connivance on the part of said accused with others in the purchase by the Fed of the U.S. Government securities to the extent of $3,000,000,000 with U.S. Government's own credit unlawfully taken, it being obvious that the Fed do no not intend to pay anything of value to the U.S. Government for the said U.S. Government securities no provision for payment in gold or lawful money appearing in the so-called Farm Relief bill- and the U.S. Government will thus be placed in a position of conferring a gift of $3,000,000,000 in the U.S. Government securities on the Fed to enable them to pay more on their bad debts to foreign governments, foreign central banks of issue, private interests, and private and commercial banks, both foreign and domestic, and the Bank of International Settlements, and

"Whereas the U.S. Government will thus go into debt to the extent of $3,000,000,000 and will then have an additional claim of $3,000,000,000 in currency unlawfully created against it and whereas no private interest should be permitted to buy U.S. Government securities with the Government's own credit unlawfully taken and whereas currency should not be issued for the benefit of said private interest or any interests on U.S. Government securities so acquired, and whereas it has been publicly stated and not denied that the inflation amendment of the Farm

Relief Act is the matter of benefit which was secured by Ramsey MacDonald, the Prime Minister of Great Britain, upon the occasion of his latest visit to the U.S. Treasury, and whereas there is grave danger that the accused will employ the provision creating U.S. Government securities to the extent of $3,000,000,000 and three millions in currency to be issuable thereupon for the benefit of themselves and their foreign principals, and that they will convert the currency so obtained to the uses of Great Britain by secret arrangements with the Bank of England of which they are the agents, and for which they maintain an account and perform services at the expense of the U.S. Treasury, and that they will likewise confer benefits upon the Bank of International Settlements for which they maintain an account and perform services at the expense of the U.S. Treasury; and

"Whereas I charge them, jointly and severally, with having concealed the insolvency of the Fed and with having failed to report the insolvency of the Fed to the Congress and with having conspired to have the said insolvent institutions continue in operation, and with having permitted the said insolvent institutions to receive U.S. Government funds and other deposits, and with having permitted them to exercise control over the gold reserves of the U.S. and with having permitted them to transfer upward of $100,000,000,000 of their debts and losses to the general public and the Government of the U.S., and with having permitted foreign debts of the Fed to be paid with the property, the savings, the wages, and the salaries of the people of the U.S. and with the farms and the homes of the American people, and whereas I charge them with forcing the bad debts of the Fed upon the general public covertly and dishonestly and and with taking the general wealth and savings of the people of the U.S. under false pretenses, to pay the debts of the Fed to foreigners; and

"Whereas I charge them, jointly and severally, with violations of the Fed Act and other laws; with maladministration of the h evasions of the Fed Law and other laws; and with having unlawfully failed to report violations of law on the part of the Fed Banks which, if known, would have caused the Fed Banks to lose their charters, and

"Whereas I charge them, jointly and severally, with failure to protect and maintain the gold reserves and the gold stock and gold coinage of the U.S. and with having sold the gold reserves of the U.S to foreign Governments, foreign central banks of issue, foreign commercial and private banks, and other foreign institutions and individuals at a profit to themselves, and I charge them with having sold gold reserves of the U.S. so that between 1924 and 1928 the U.S. gained no gold on net account but suffered a decline in its percentage of central gold reserves from the 45.9 percent in 1924 to 37.5 percent in 1928 notwithstanding the fact that the U.S. had a favorable balance of trade throughout that period, and

"Whereas I charge them, jointly and severally, with having conspired to concentrate U.S. Government securities and thus the national debt of the U.S. in the hands of foreigners and international money lenders and with having conspired to transfer to foreigners and international money lenders title to and control of the financial resources of the U.S.; and

"Whereas I charge them, jointly and severally, with having fictitiously paid installments on the national debt with Government credit unlawfully taken; and

"Whereas I charge them, jointly and severally, with the loss of the U.S. Government funds entrusted to their care; and

"Whereas I charge them, jointly and severally, with having destroyed independent banks in the U.S. and with having thereby caused losses amounting to billions of dollars to the said banks, and to the general public of the U.S., and

"Whereas I charge them, jointly and severally, with the failure to furnish true reports of the business operations and the true conditions of the Fed to the Congress and the people, and having furnished false and misleading reports to the congress of the U.S., and

"Whereas I charge them, jointly and severally, with having published false and misleading propaganda intended to deceive the American people and to cause the U.S. to lose its independence; and

"Whereas I charge them, jointly and severally, with unlawfully allowing Great Britain to share in the profits of the Fed at the expense of the Government and the people of the U.S.; and

"Whereas I charge them, jointly and severally, with having entered into secret agreements and illegal transactions with Montague Norman, Governor of the Bank of England; and

"Whereas I charge them, jointly and severally, with swindling the U.S. Treasury and the people of the U.S. in pretending to have received payment from Great Britain of the amount due on the British ware debt to the U.S. in December, 1932; and

"Whereas I charge them, jointly and severally, with having conspired with their foreign principals and others to defraud the U.S. Government and to prevent the people of the U.S. from receiving payment of the war debts due to the U.S. from foreign nations; and

"Whereas I charge them, jointly and severally, with having robbed the U.S Government and the people of the U.S. by their theft and sale of the gold reserves of the U.S. and other unlawful transactions created a deficit in the U.S. Treasury, which has necessitated to a large extent the destruction of our national defense and the reduction of the U.S. Army and the U.S. Navy and other branches of the national defense; and

"Whereas I charge them, jointly and severally, of having reduced the U.S. from a first class power to one that is dependent, and with having reduced the U.S. from a rich and powerful nation to one that is internationally poor; and
"Whereas I charge them, jointly and severally, with the crime of having treasonable conspired and acted against the peace and security of the U.S. and with having treasonable conspired to destroy constitutional Government in the U.S.

"Resolve, That the Committee on the Judiciary is authorized and directed as a whole or by subcommittee, to investigate the official conduct of the Fed agents to determine whether, in the opinion of the said committee, they have been guilty of any high crime or misdemeanor which in the contemplation the Constitution requires the interposition of the Constitutional powers of the

House. Such Committee shall report its finding to the House, together with such resolution or resolutions of impeachment or other recommendations as it deems proper.

"For the purpose of this resolution the Committee is authorized to sit and act during the present Congress at such times and places in the District of Columbia or elsewhere, whether or not the House is sitting, has recessed or has adjourned, to hold such clerical, stenographic, and other assistants, to require of such witnesses and the production of such books, papers, and documents, to take such testimony, to have such printing and binding done, and to make such expenditures as it deems necessary."

Enoch Powell

Rivers of Blood

What follows is Enoch Powell's so-called 'Rivers of Blood' speech. This oddly prescient speech was delivered to a Conservative Association meeting in Birmingham (UK) on April 20, 1968.

The supreme function of statesmanship is to provide against preventable evils. In seeking to do so, it encounters obstacles which are deeply rooted in human nature.

One is that by the very order of things such evils are not demonstrable until they have occurred: at each stage in their onset there is room for doubt and for dispute whether they be real or imaginary. By the same token, they attract little attention in comparison with current troubles, which are both indisputable and pressing: whence the besetting temptation of all politics to concern itself with the immediate present at the expense of the future.

Above all, people are disposed to mistake predicting troubles for causing troubles and even for desiring troubles: "If only," they love to think, "if only people wouldn't talk about it, it probably wouldn't happen."

Perhaps this habit goes back to the primitive belief that the word and the thing, the name and the object, are identical.

At all events, the discussion of future grave but, with effort now, avoidable evils is the most unpopular and at the same time the most necessary occupation for the politician. Those who knowingly shirk it deserve, and not infrequently receive, the curses of those who come after.

A week or two ago I fell into conversation with a constituent, a middle-aged, quite ordinary working man employed in one of our nationalised industries.

After a sentence or two about the weather, he suddenly said: "If I had the money to go, I wouldn't stay in this country." I made some deprecatory reply to the effect that even this government wouldn't last for ever; but he took no notice, and continued: "I have three children, all of them been through grammar school and two of them married now, with family. I shan't be satisfied till I have seen them all settled overseas. In this country in 15 or 20 years' time the black man will have the whip hand over the white man."

I can already hear the chorus of execration. How dare I say such a horrible thing? How dare I stir up trouble and inflame feelings by repeating such a conversation?

The answer is that I do not have the right not to do so. Here is a decent, ordinary fellow Englishman, who in broad daylight in my own town says to me, his Member of Parliament, that his country will not be worth living in for his children.

I simply do not have the right to shrug my shoulders and think about something else. What he is saying, thousands and hundreds of thousands are saying and thinking – not throughout Great Britain, perhaps, but in the areas that are already undergoing the total transformation to which there is no parallel in a thousand years of English history.

In 15 or 20 years, on present trends, there will be in this country three and a half million Commonwealth immigrants and their descendants. That is not my figure. That is the official figure given to parliament by the spokesman of the Registrar General's Office.

There is no comparable official figure for the year 2000, but it must be in the region of five to seven million, approximately one-tenth of the whole population, and approaching that of Greater London. Of course, it will not be evenly distributed from Margate to Aberystwyth and from Penzance to Aberdeen. Whole areas, towns and parts of towns across England will be occupied by sections of the immigrant and immigrant-descended population.

As time goes on, the proportion of this total who are immigrant descendants, those born in England, who arrived here by exactly the same route as the rest of us, will rapidly increase. Already by 1985 the native-born would constitute the majority. It is this fact which creates the extreme urgency of action now, of just that kind of action which is hardest for politicians to take, action where the difficulties lie in the present but the evils to be prevented or minimised lie several parliaments ahead.

The natural and rational first question with a nation confronted by such a prospect is to ask: "How can its dimensions be reduced?" Granted it be not wholly preventable, can it be limited, bearing in mind that numbers are of the essence: the significance and consequences of an alien element introduced into a country or population are profoundly different according to whether that element is 1 per cent or 10 per cent.

The answers to the simple and rational question are equally simple and rational: by stopping, or virtually stopping, further inflow, and by promoting the maximum outflow. Both answers are part of the official policy of the Conservative Party.

It almost passes belief that at this moment 20 or 30 additional immigrant children are arriving from overseas in Wolverhampton alone every week – and that means 15 or 20 additional families a decade or two hence. Those whom the gods wish to destroy, they first make mad. We must be mad, literally mad, as a nation to be permitting the annual inflow of some 50,000 dependants, who are for the most part the material of the future growth of the immigrant-descended population. It is like watching a nation busily engaged in heaping up its own funeral pyre. So insane are we that we actually permit unmarried persons to immigrate for the purpose of founding a family with spouses and fiancés whom they have never seen.

Let no one suppose that the flow of dependants will automatically tail off. On the contrary, even at the present admission rate of only 5,000 a year by voucher, there is sufficient for a further

25,000 dependants per annum ad infinitum, without taking into account the huge reservoir of existing relations in this country – and I am making no allowance at all for fraudulent entry. In these circumstances nothing will suffice but that the total inflow for settlement should be reduced at once to negligible proportions, and that the necessary legislative and administrative measures be taken without delay.

I stress the words "for settlement." This has nothing to do with the entry of Commonwealth citizens, any more than of aliens, into this country, for the purposes of study or of improving their qualifications, like (for instance) the Commonwealth doctors who, to the advantage of their own countries, have enabled our hospital service to be expanded faster than would otherwise have been possible. They are not, and never have been, immigrants.

I turn to re-emigration. If all immigration ended tomorrow, the rate of growth of the immigrant and immigrant-descended population would be substantially reduced, but the prospective size of this element in the population would still leave the basic character of the national danger unaffected. This can only be tackled while a considerable proportion of the total still comprises persons who entered this country during the last ten years or so.

Hence the urgency of implementing now the second element of the Conservative Party's policy: the encouragement of re-emigration.

Nobody can make an estimate of the numbers which, with generous assistance, would choose either to return to their countries of origin or to go to other countries anxious to receive the manpower and the skills they represent.

Nobody knows, because no such policy has yet been attempted. I can only say that, even at present, immigrants in my own constituency from time to time come to me, asking if I can find them assistance to return home. If such a policy were adopted and pursued with the determination which the gravity of the alternative justifies, the resultant outflow could appreciably alter the prospects.

The third element of the Conservative Party's policy is that all who are in this country as citizens should be equal before the law and that there shall be no discrimination or difference made between them by public authority. As Mr Heath has put it we will have no "first-class citizens" and "second-class citizens." This does not mean that the immigrant and his descendent should be elevated into a privileged or special class or that the citizen should be denied his right to discriminate in the management of his own affairs between one fellow-citizen and another or that he should be subjected to imposition as to his reasons and motive for behaving in one lawful manner rather than another.

There could be no grosser misconception of the realities than is entertained by those who vociferously demand legislation as they call it "against discrimination", whether they be leader-writers of the same kidney and sometimes on the same newspapers which year after year in the 1930s tried to blind this country to the rising peril which confronted it, or archbishops who live in palaces, faring delicately with the bedclothes pulled right up over their heads. They have got it exactly and diametrically wrong.

The discrimination and the deprivation, the sense of alarm and of resentment, lies not with the immigrant population but with those among whom they have come and are still coming.

This is why to enact legislation of the kind before parliament at this moment is to risk throwing a match on to gunpowder. The kindest thing that can be said about those who propose and support it is that they know not what they do.

Nothing is more misleading than comparison between the Commonwealth immigrant in Britain and the American Negro. The Negro population of the United States, which was already in existence before the United States became a nation, started literally as slaves and were later given the franchise and other rights of citizenship, to the exercise of which they have only gradually and still incompletely come. The Commonwealth immigrant came to Britain as a full citizen, to a country which knew no discrimination between one citizen and another, and he entered instantly into the possession of the rights of every citizen, from the vote to free treatment under the National Health Service.

Whatever drawbacks attended the immigrants arose not from the law or from public policy or from administration, but from those personal circumstances and accidents which cause, and always will cause, the fortunes and experience of one man to be different from another's.

But while, to the immigrant, entry to this country was admission to privileges and opportunities eagerly sought, the impact upon the existing population was very different. For reasons which they could not comprehend, and in pursuance of a decision by default, on which they were never consulted, they found themselves made strangers in their own country.

They found their wives unable to obtain hospital beds in childbirth, their children unable to obtain school places, their homes and neighbourhoods changed beyond recognition, their plans and prospects for the future defeated; at work they found that employers hesitated to apply to the immigrant worker the standards of discipline and competence required of the native-born worker; they began to hear, as time went by, more and more voices which told them that they were now the unwanted. They now learn that a one-way privilege is to be established by act of parliament; a law which cannot, and is not intended to, operate to protect them or redress their grievances is to be enacted to give the stranger, the disgruntled and the agent-provocateur the power to pillory them for their private actions.

In the hundreds upon hundreds of letters I received when I last spoke on this subject two or three months ago, there was one striking feature which was largely new and which I find ominous. All Members of Parliament are used to the typical anonymous correspondent; but what surprised and alarmed me was the high proportion of ordinary, decent, sensible people, writing a rational and often well-educated letter, who believed that they had to omit their address because it was dangerous to have committed themselves to paper to a Member of Parliament agreeing with the views I had expressed, and that they would risk penalties or reprisals if they were known to have done so. The sense of being a persecuted minority which is growing among ordinary English people in the areas of the country which are affected is something that those without direct experience can hardly imagine.

I am going to allow just one of those hundreds of people to speak for me:

"Eight years ago in a respectable street in Wolverhampton a house was sold to a Negro. Now only one white (a woman old-age pensioner) lives there. This is her story. She lost her husband and both her sons in the war. So she turned her seven-roomed house, her only asset, into a boarding house. She worked hard and did well, paid off her mortgage and began to put something by for her old age. Then the immigrants moved in. With growing fear, she saw one house after another taken over. The quiet street became a place of noise and confusion. Regretfully, her white tenants moved out.

"The day after the last one left, she was awakened at 7am by two Negroes who wanted to use her 'phone to contact their employer. When she refused, as she would have refused any stranger at such an hour, she was abused and feared she would have been attacked but for the chain on her door. Immigrant families have tried to rent rooms in her house, but she always refused. Her little store of money went, and after paying rates, she has less than £2 per week. "She went to apply for a rate reduction and was seen by a young girl, who on hearing she had a seven-roomed house, suggested she should let part of it. When she said the only people she could get were Negroes, the girl said, "Racial prejudice won't get you anywhere in this country." So she went home.

"The telephone is her lifeline. Her family pay the bill, and help her out as best they can. Immigrants have offered to buy her house – at a price which the prospective landlord would be able to recover from his tenants in weeks, or at most a few months. She is becoming afraid to go out. Windows are broken. She finds excreta pushed through her letter box. When she goes to the shops, she is followed by children, charming, wide-grinning piccaninnies. They cannot speak English, but one word they know. "Racialist," they chant. When the new Race Relations Bill is passed, this woman is convinced she will go to prison. And is she so wrong? I begin to wonder."

The other dangerous delusion from which those who are wilfully or otherwise blind to realities suffer, is summed up in the word "integration." To be integrated into a population means to become for all practical purposes indistinguishable from its other members.

Now, at all times, where there are marked physical differences, especially of colour, integration is difficult though, over a period, not impossible. There are among the Commonwealth immigrants who have come to live here in the last fifteen years or so, many thousands whose wish and purpose is to be integrated and whose every thought and endeavour is bent in that direction.
But to imagine that such a thing enters the heads of a great and growing majority of immigrants and their descendants is a ludicrous misconception, and a dangerous one.

We are on the verge here of a change. Hitherto it has been force of circumstance and of background which has rendered the very idea of integration inaccessible to the greater part of the immigrant population – that they never conceived or intended such a thing, and that their numbers and physical concentration meant the pressures towards integration which normally bear upon any small minority did not operate.

Now we are seeing the growth of positive forces acting against integration, of vested interests in the preservation and sharpening of racial and religious differences, with a view to the exercise of actual domination, first over fellow-immigrants and then over the rest of the population. The cloud no bigger than a man's hand, that can so rapidly overcast the sky, has been visible recently in Wolverhampton and has shown signs of spreading quickly. The words I am about to use, verbatim as they appeared in the local press on 17 February, are not mine, but those of a Labour Member of Parliament who is a minister in the present government:

'The Sikh communities' campaign to maintain customs inappropriate in Britain is much to be regretted. Working in Britain, particularly in the public services, they should be prepared to accept the terms and conditions of their employment. To claim special communal rights (or should one say rites?) leads to a dangerous fragmentation within society. This communalism is a canker; whether practised by one colour or another it is to be strongly condemned.'

All credit to John Stonehouse for having had the insight to perceive that, and the courage to say it.

For these dangerous and divisive elements the legislation proposed in the Race Relations Bill is the very pabulum they need to flourish. Here is the means of showing that the immigrant communities can organise to consolidate their members, to agitate and campaign against their fellow citizens, and to overawe and dominate the rest with the legal weapons which the ignorant and the ill-informed have provided. As I look ahead,

I am filled with foreboding; like the Roman, I seem to see "the River Tiber foaming with much blood."

That tragic and intractable phenomenon which we watch with horror on the other side of the Atlantic but which there is interwoven with the history and existence of the States itself, is coming upon us here by our own volition and our own neglect. Indeed, it has all but come. In numerical terms, it will be of American proportions long before the end of the century.

Only resolute and urgent action will avert it even now. Whether there will be the public will to demand and obtain that action, I do not know. All I know is that to see, and not to speak, would be the great betrayal.

Such prophecies can only be fulfilled if we do nothing.
~ Rachel Summers